GCSE English Literature AQA Anthology

The Study Guide

Poems from

Heaney, Clarke, pre-1914

AQA A Specification — Higher Level

This book is a step-by-step guide to becoming an expert on the Anthology part of your GCSE English Literature exam.

It's got everything you need to know — annotated poems, exam themes and worked essays.

It's ideal for use as a classroom study book or a revision guide.

What CGP is all about

Our sole aim here at CGP is to produce the highest quality books — carefully written, immaculately presented and dangerously close to being funny.

Then we work our socks off to get them out to you — at the cheapest possible prices.

Contents

Section One — Pre-1914 Poetry Bank

Section Two — Seamus Heaney

Section Three — Gillian Clarke

Section Four — Themes: Ideas, Attitudes and Feelings

Section Five — Themes: Methods of Poetry

Section Six — How to Answer the Question

☆ = Key poems as suggested by AQA

Published by Coordination Group Publications Ltd.

Editors:
Charley Darbishire, Kate Houghton, Katherine Reed, Edward Robinson, Jennifer Underwood.

Contributors:
Margaret Giordmaine, Roland Haynes, Shelagh Moore, Elisabeth Sanderson, Nicola Woodfin.

With thanks to Kate Houghton and Anne Thomas for the proofreading.

ISBN: 978 1 84146 889 1

Groovy website: www.cgpbooks.co.uk
Jolly bits of clipart from CorelDRAW®
Printed by Elanders Hindson Ltd, Newcastle upon Tyne.

How To Use This Book

This book will help you do better in your GCSE English Literature Anthology Exam. It's full of straightforward ways of getting extra marks. Start by asking your teacher which poems and themes you need to study: some schools get you to study all of them, others pick out certain ones.

There are Six Sections in this book

Sections One, Two and Three are about the Poems

There are two pages about each poem. This is what the pages look like:

There's a nice picture of the poet and some info about their life.

Important or tricky bits of the poem are highlighted and explained.

Difficult words are defined in the poem dictionary.

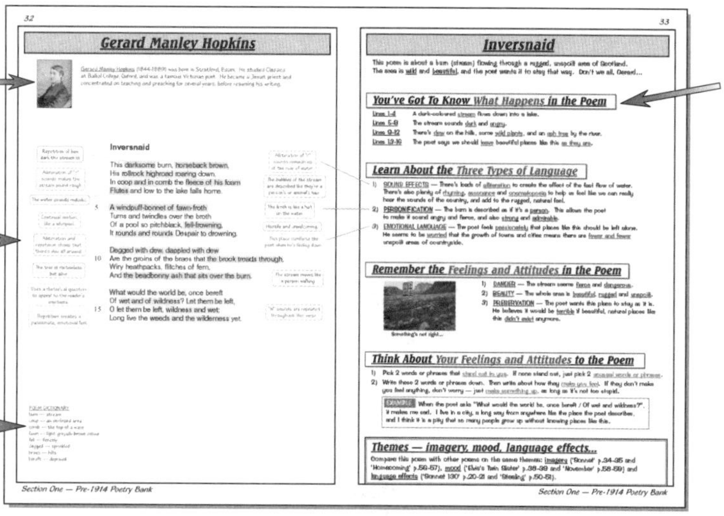

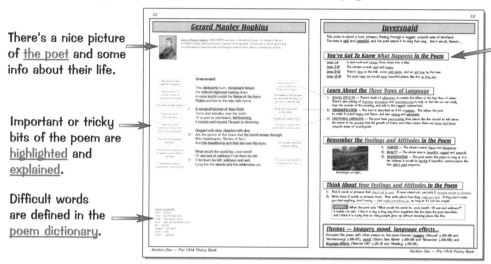

On the right-hand page there are notes about the poem. They include:

- what happens in the poem.
- the language the poet uses.
- the feelings of the poet.
- a bit that will help you to write about how you feel about the poem.

Read through the pages on the poems you've been told to study. When you've read about each poem, shut the book and write out as much as you can remember. See what you've left out, then do it again.

Sections Four and Five are about the Themes

In the exam, you'll have to compare how four poems relate to one of the themes. In Sections Four and Five, there's a page about each of the main themes that might come up. The pages tell you which poems use each theme and how different poets treat the same theme. Read them, understand them and learn them.

Section Six is About Preparing for your Exam

Pages 84-85 tell you how to plan and write good essays using CGP's 5-step method. The section also includes exam questions with sample answers. This is what they look like:

Sample exam question.

Sample plan for how you could answer the exam question.

A sample student answer, which continues on the opposite page.

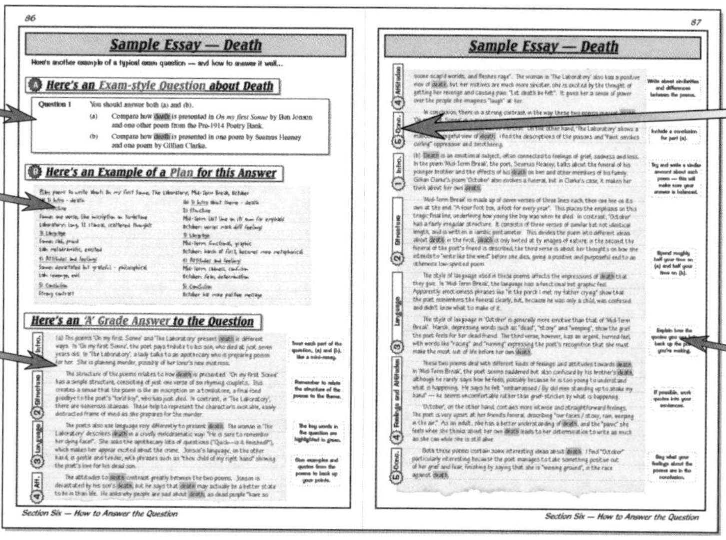

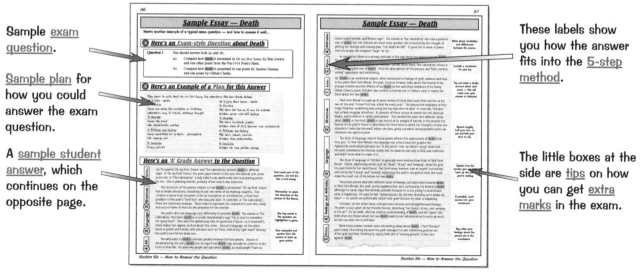

These labels show you how the answer fits into the 5-step method.

The little boxes at the side are tips on how you can get extra marks in the exam.

Write some essays using the 5-step method. Use the exam-style questions in CGP's higher-level Heaney and Clarke Anthology Workbook, if you have it, or ask your teacher for some practice questions. You get one hour to answer the question in the exam, so practise doing some timed essays.

Key Poem

Ben Jonson

Ben Jonson (1572-1637) was the son of a clergyman. He attended Westminster School, before becoming a bricklayer and later joining the army. He went on to become one of the most important poets of his time. He also wrote plays, and was a friend of William Shakespeare.

On my first Sonne

Farewell, thou child of my right hand, and joy;
My sinne was too much hope of thee, lov'd boy,
Seven yeeres tho'wert lent to me, and I thee pay,
Exacted by thy fate, on the just day.
O, could I loose all father, now. For why
Will man lament the state he should envie?
To have so soone scap'd worlds, and fleshes rage,
And, if no other miserie, yet age?
Rest in soft peace, and, ask'd, say here doth lye
Ben. Jonson his best piece of poetrie.
For whose sake, hence-forth, all his vowes be such,
As what he loves may never like too much.

The poem is written directly to his son. It's his way of saying a fond goodbye.

His "sinne" was hoping that his son would live for a long time.

Suggests that he thinks that his son's death was inevitable and something he could not control.

Jonson seems to want to be dead too.

Shows his affection for his son.

His son was his greatest creation.

He decides he'll never love anyone else so dearly because he doesn't want to feel so much pain again.

He loved his son very much.

Uses money as a metaphor. Jonson's son was "lent" to him for seven years and now he has to "pay" his debt through the death of his son.

Says there are advantages of being dead, e.g. you don't have to suffer pain and old age.

This type of language is usually found on a gravestone — the poem commemorates Jonson's son.

POEM DICTIONARY
sinne — an old way of spelling sin
yeeres — years
tho'wert — you were
lament — to feel sorrow or regret
scap'd — a shortened way of writing escaped
miserie — an old way of spelling misery
hence-forth — from now on

On my first Sonne

Key Poem

This is a simple poem about a father who is mourning the death of his seven year-old son. The poem is the father's way of saying goodbye to his son.

You've Got To Know What Happens in the Poem

Lines 1-4 The man says goodbye to his seven year old son who has just died.

Lines 5-8 He says he envies his son because in heaven you don't have to deal with all the horrible things that happen in life.

Lines 9-12 Ben Jonson says that his son was his best ever creation. He decides that in the future he won't love anyone as much as he loved his son so that he won't get so upset if they die.

Learn About the Three Types of Language

1) PRIDE and AFFECTION — The poet is very fond of his son. The poem is written as though he's talking directly to him. This makes it seem very personal and helps you to imagine the poet's feelings.
2) METAPHORICAL LANGUAGE — A metaphor about debt and money explains why his son died.
3) COMMENTS ABOUT DEATH — There are quite a few different ideas about death in this poem. On one hand the poet is sad that his son's dead, on the other he says that early death isn't all bad because you don't have to grow old and suffer pain.

Remember the Feelings and Attitudes in the Poem

1) GRIEF — The poet is really upset about the death of his son.
2) UNCERTAINTY — The poet wonders whether it is better to be dead than to be alive.
3) PAIN — He's so devastated by his son's death that he decides never to love anyone else as much, because he doesn't want to suffer like this again.

Think About Your Feelings and Attitudes to the Poem

1) Pick 2 words or phrases that stand out to you. If none stand out, just pick 2 unusual words or phrases.
2) Write these 2 words or phrases down. Then write about how they make you feel. If they don't make you feel anything, don't worry — just make something up, as long as it's not too stupid.

EXAMPLE I find it very touching that the poet describes his son as his "best piece of poetrie". Even though he was one of the best poets of his time, he thinks that having a son was a greater achievement than his writing.

Themes — death, parent/child relationships, love...

Compare 'On my first Sonne' with other poems about the same themes: death ('Mid-Term Break' p.46-47, 'October' p.62-63), parent/child relationships ('Catrin' p.52-53 and 'The Affliction of Margaret' p.10-11) and love ('Sonnet 130' p.20-21 and 'Mali' p.56-57).

William Butler Yeats

William Butler Yeats (1865-1939) was born in Dublin. He is often considered to be Ireland's greatest ever poet. As well as poetry, Yeats wrote many plays and won the Nobel Prize for Literature. He was also involved in the Celtic Revival, a movement to encourage traditional Irish culture and discourage English influences on Ireland.

The Song of the Old Mother

I rise in the dawn, and I kneel and blow
Till the seed of the fire flicker and glow;
And then I must scrub and bake and sweep
Till stars are beginning to blink and peep;
And the young lie long and dream in their bed
Of the matching of ribbons for bosom and head,
And their day goes over in idleness,
And they sigh if the wind but lift a tress:
While I must work because I am old,
And the seed of the fire gets feeble and cold.

Shows the poem is from the point of view of the old mother.

The old woman gets up really early whilst the young people lie about in bed — this is emphasised by alliteration.

Young people are only concerned by trivial matters.

The woman thinks that young people are always moaning about things that aren't important.

Suggests that the woman has no choice.

The woman gets the fire going in the morning, but by the end of the day it's going out — she'll have to do it all again the next day. This emphasises how boring and repetitive her life is.

The woman's work makes her tired and weak, just as the fire gets weaker as the day goes on.

The poem is in rhyming couplets.

List of all the rubbish jobs that the old woman has to do.

Slow, plodding rhythm suggests the boring, repetitive tasks.

Use of 'their' and 'I' emphasises the differences between the old woman and the young people.

Fire going out could be a symbol for her life coming to an end.

POEM DICTIONARY
tress — a lock of hair

The Song of the Old Mother

In this poem an old woman describes the daily chores she has to do. She seems to think that people in younger generations are a bit lazy and that they have a much easier life than she does.

You've Got To Know What Happens in the Poem

Lines 1-2 — The old woman gets up and gets the fire going.
Lines 3-4 — She does cooking and cleaning until night time.
Lines 5-8 — The woman thinks that younger people (possibly her children) are lazy and that they don't have to do as much hard work as she has to.
Line 9-10 — The woman summarises her attitude to life and the fire she has made starts to go out.

Learn About the Two Types of Language

1) RHYMING COUPLETS AND RHYTHM — the rhyming couplets make the poem sound repetitive like the woman's work. The regular rhythm also makes the poem read like a song which ties in with the title of the poem.
2) CONTRAST — Yeats points out all the differences between the life that the old woman lives and the lives of the young people using lists and descriptions of their daily activities and thoughts.

Remember the Feelings and Attitudes in the Poem

1) SYMPATHY — The poet feels sorry for the old mother.
2) DRUDGERY — The poet thinks that the woman's life will inevitably carry on like this until she dies.
3) MORAL — Yeats uses the poem to show people what life is like for old people who have to do lots of work — perhaps he hopes that it will change people's attitudes towards poor elderly people.

Think About Your Feelings and Attitudes to the Poem

1) Pick 2 words or phrases that stand out to you. If none stand out, just pick 2 unusual words or phrases.
2) Write these 2 words or phrases down. Then write about how they make you feel. If they don't make you feel anything, don't worry — just make something up, as long as it's not too stupid.

EXAMPLE The phrase "lie long and dream in their bed" makes me feel sympathy for the woman in the poem and anger towards the idle young people. The phrase highlights the stark difference between the lives of the young people and the old woman's life.

Themes — attitudes to others, first person, imagery...

Compare 'The Song of the Old Mother' with other poems about the same themes: attitudes to others ('The Affliction of Margaret' p.10-11 and 'The Laboratory' p.30-31), use of the first person ('Mid-Term Break' p.46-47) and imagery ('Tichborne's Elegy' p.14-15 and 'October' p.62-63).

THIS IS A FLAP. FOLD THIS PAGE OUT.

Key Poem

William Wordsworth

William Wordsworth (1770-1850) was one of England's greatest poets. He was born in Cockermouth, and wrote many poems about the Lake District. He went to Cambridge University. He was made Poet Laureate in 1843.

The Affliction of Margaret

Margaret addresses her son directly in the first stanza.

She's looking for answers, trying to make sense of her son's disappearance.

She's desperate to find him, whether he's rich, poor or dead.

Where art thou, my beloved Son,
Where art thou, worse to me than dead?
Oh find me, prosperous or undone!
Or, if the grave be now thy bed,
Why am I ignorant of the same
That I may rest; and neither blame,
Nor sorrow may attend thy name?

Her tone is now more reflective, rather than questioning.

Her pain seems to last an eternity.

Her lack of knowledge.

Seven years, alas! to have received
No tidings of an only child;
To have despaired, and have believed,
And be for evermore beguiled;
Sometimes with thoughts of very bliss!
I catch at them, and then I miss;
Was ever darkness like to this?

She remembers only the best things about him.

She won't accept any criticism of him.

He was among the prime in worth,
An object beauteous to behold;
Well born, well bred; I sent him forth
Ingenuous, innocent, and bold:
If things ensued that wanted grace,
As hath been said, they were not base;
And never blush was on my face.

Even playful cries worry a mother — so her pain now must be unbearable.

This fits in with the idea of innocence in the previous verse.

Ah! little doth the Young One dream,
When full of play and childish cares,
What power hath even his wildest scream,
Heard by his Mother unawares!
He knows it not, he cannot guess:
Years to a Mother bring distress;
But do not make her love the less.

She's struggling to control her emotions.

She knows she's being irrational.

Simile creates a sense of gentle but constant crying.

She's suffered on her own.

Neglect me! no I suffered long
From that ill thought; and being blind,
Said, 'Pride shall help me in my wrong;
Kind mother have I been, as kind
As ever breathed:' and that is true;
I've wet my path with tears like dew,
Weeping for him when no one knew.

William Wordsworth

Talks to him directly again.

Nothing but her son matters to her now, she doesn't care whether he is rich or poor.

My Son, if thou be humbled, poor,
Hopeless of honour and of gain,
Oh! do not dread thy mother's door;
Think not of me with grief and pain:
I now can see with better eyes;
And worldly grandeur I despise,
And fortune with her gifts and lies.

She thinks that birds have fate on their side — but she doesn't.

She thinks there's no chance of her wishes coming true.

Alas! the fowls of Heaven have wings,
And blasts of Heaven will aid their flight;
They mount – how short a voyage brings
The Wanderers back to their delight!
Chains tie us down by land and sea;
And wishes, vain as mine, may be
All that is left to comfort thee.

Similarity of the words suggests these ideas are leaping into her head without much thought.

Words of pain and torture — she can only imagine the worst in this verse.

Perhaps some dungeon hears thee groan,
Maimed, mangled by inhuman men;
Or thou upon a Desart thrown
Inheritest the Lion's Den;
Or hast been summon'd to the Deep,
Thou, Thou, and all thy mates, to keep
An incommunicable sleep.

A desperate and irrational way of trying to deal with her situation.

Her greatest fear is not being able to talk to him.

She seems to worship him.

I look for Ghosts; but none will force
Their way to me; 'tis falsely said
That there was ever intercourse
Betwixt the living and the dead;
For, surely, then I should have sight
Of Him I wait for day and night,
With love and longings infinite.

Her worries come to her randomly — she can't control her thoughts.

Her anxiety has sapped all her strength.

She can't be happy about anything — she seems to be obsessed.

My apprehensions come in crowds;
I dread the rustling of the grass;
The very shadows of the clouds
Have power to shake me as they pass;
I question things, and do not find
One that will answer to my mind;
And all the world appears unkind.

She feels that no one could understand how strong her grief is.

Beyond participation lie
My troubles, and beyond relief:
If any chance to heave a sigh
They pity me, and not my grief.
Then come to me, my Son, or send
Some tidings that my woes may end;
I have no other earthly friend.

POEM DICTIONARY
affliction — pain
beguiled — fooled
ingenuous — open, honest
ensued — followed
base — bad, corrupt
incommunicable — too far away to talk with
intercourse — conversation
betwixt — between
apprehensions — fears
tidings — news

The Affliction of Margaret

Key Poem

The poet describes the feelings of Margaret, a woman whose son has been missing for seven years. She fears the worst, and she's desperate to talk to him.

You've Got To Know What Happens in the Poem

Lines 1-14	Margaret describes the pain of not knowing where her son is.
Lines 15-21	She goes on about how good-looking and well-meaning her son was.
Lines 22-28	She says children don't realise how much their mothers worry about them.
Lines 29-42	Margaret says she was a good mother. She wants her son to return, whatever state he's in.
Lines 43-49	She says that birds have wings, so they're free to return. People don't have this freedom.
Lines 50-56	She imagines terrible things happening to her son, like being imprisoned or shipwrecked.
Lines 57-70	She says it's impossible to talk to the dead. There's no escape from her fears.
Lines 71-77	No-one can understand her grief. Her son returning to her is the only way to end it.

Learn About the Three Types of Language

1) OBSESSIVE LANGUAGE — Thoughts of Margaret's son have completely taken over her life. Her thoughts are illogical, and she feels she can't be happy about anything while her son's still missing.
2) PAIN and FEAR — She seems to torture herself by thinking of all the awful things that might have happened to him. She feels that it would be better to know he was dead than not to know anything.
3) REFLECTIVE LANGUAGE — She's sometimes more reasoning, trying to find answers. She feels she can't explain her feelings to anyone — she's alone with her sorrow, and desperate just to talk to her son.

Remember the Feelings and Attitudes in the Poem

"I hope he's got some clean underpants..."

1) SYMPATHY — The poet feels sorry for Margaret.
2) ANXIETY — He shows how anxious she is to find out how her son is.
3) DESPERATION — She feels absolutely desperate — nothing matters to her but her son.

Margaret's quite irrational at times — she tries to talk to her son even though he's not there, and her mind jumps from one thought to another fairly randomly.

Think About Your Feelings and Attitudes to the Poem

1) Pick 2 words or phrases that stand out to you. If none stand out, just pick 2 unusual words or phrases.
2) Write these 2 words or phrases down. Then write about how they make you feel. If they don't make you feel anything, don't worry — just make something up, as long as it's not too stupid.

EXAMPLE The phrase "I've wet my path with tears like dew" makes me feel great sorrow for the mother. It seems there is no end to her suffering, and her pain follows her wherever she goes.

Themes — parent/child relationship, strong emotions, love...

Compare 'The Affliction of Margaret' with other poems about the same themes: parent/child relationships ('Follower' p.50-51 and 'Catrin' p.52-53), strong emotions ('The Laboratory' p.30-31 and 'The Field-Mouse' p.60-61) and love ('Mali' p.56-57 and 'Catrin' p.52-53).

William Blake

William Blake (1757-1827) was born in London, and educated at home by his mother. He was a poet, artist, engraver and publisher. He believed in the power of the imagination and religion over materialism.

The lost child could be a metaphor for someone who's lost their faith.

The Little Boy Lost

The boy calls after his dad, but "father" could also mean God.

'Father, father, where are you going?
Oh do not walk so fast!
Speak, father, speak to your little boy
Or else I shall be lost.'

He's lost and can't see his way without God to guide him.

The boy sounds desperate and helpless.

The night was dark, no father was there,
The child was wet with dew;
The mire was deep, and the child did weep,
And away the vapour flew.

The child seems doomed on his own.

Could be some kind of guiding light or spirit.

As well as being found, this could mean someone who's found their faith again.

The Little Boy Found

This can be interpreted in different ways. The light could be like the star that led the wise men to the baby Jesus. Or it could be a bad spirit that is leading the little boy into danger.

The little boy lost in the lonely fen,
Led by the wand'ring light,
Began to cry; but God, ever nigh,
Appeared like his father in white.

Suggests God is always there for you when you need him.

God is a much better father to the boy than his actual father.

He kissed the child, and by the hand led,
And to his mother brought,
Who in sorrow pale, through the lonely dale
Her little boy weeping sought.

God shows the boy the way home — compare this with line 5 above.

The boy's mum seems devoted and loving — unlike his dad who failed to look after him.

The mother has been crying, just like the boy.

POEM DICTIONARY
mire — mud
fen — a marshy area
nigh — near
dale — a valley in a hilly area

The Little Boy Lost and *The Little Boy Found*

These two poems go together to tell a sweet little tale about a little boy who gets lost... and then gets found again, with a bit of help from God. The poems have a religious message — the poet says that God will show us the way when we're lost.

You've Got To Know What Happens in the Poems

The Little Boy Lost

Lines 1-4 A little boy calls out to his dad, asking him to wait so he doesn't get lost.

Lines 5-8 But his dad disappears, leaving the boy lost and crying in the rain.

The Little Boy Found

Lines 1-4 The boy's lost on his own, but luckily for him God shows up.

Lines 5-8 God leads the boy back to his mum, who was out looking for him.

Learn About the Two Types of Language

1) EMOTIVE LANGUAGE — The poet's descriptions of the boy make him seem helpless and vulnerable. This makes the reader pity him. It also shows how he can't cope on his own.
2) RELIGIOUS LANGUAGE — There's lots of Christian imagery in the poem. This supports the overall religious message — that we are lost without God, and can only find safety with his help.

Remember the Feelings and Attitudes in the Poems

These two poems are a bit boring, so here's a picture of something more exciting.

1) FEAR — The boy is desperate and scared.
2) CONCERN — His mother is worried sick about her son.
3) RELIGION — The poet believes people are only safe when they're with God. He thinks people are lost without God.

Think About Your Feelings and Attitudes to the Poems

1) Pick 2 words or phrases that stand out to you. If none stand out, just pick 2 unusual words or phrases.
2) Write these 2 words or phrases down. Then write about how they make you feel. If they don't make you feel anything, don't worry — just make something up, as long as it's not too stupid.

EXAMPLE When the child says "Speak, father, speak to your little boy", I feel really sorry for him. He seems completely helpless and unable to survive on his own.

Themes — danger, strong emotions, imagery...

Compare 'The Little Boy Lost'/'The Little Boy Found' with other poems about the same themes: danger ('The Field-Mouse' p.60-61 and 'Patrolling Barnegat' p.18-19), strong emotions ('The Affliction of Margaret' p.10-11) and imagery ('Storm on the Island' p.48-49 and 'Cold Knap Lake' p.66-67).

Chidiock Tichborne

Chidiock Tichborne (c.1558-1586) was a Roman Catholic. He was part of a plot to murder Elizabeth I and replace her with the Catholic Mary Queen of Scots. The plot was discovered and Chidiock was arrested and condemned to death. He wrote this poem in a letter to his wife, Agnes, just before his death. He was hung, drawn and quartered in 1586, at the age of 28.

Tichborne's Elegy

Written with his own hand in the Tower before his execution

My prime of youth is but a frost of cares,
My feast of joy is but a dish of pain;
My crop of corn is but a field of tares,
And all my good is but vain hope of gain.
The day is past, and yet I saw no sun;
And now I live, and now my life is done.

My tale was heard, and yet it was not told,
My fruit is fallen, and yet my leaves are green;
My youth is spent, and yet I am not old,
I saw the world, and yet I was not seen.
My thread is cut, and yet it is not spun;
And now I live, and now my life is done.

I sought my death, and found it in my womb,
I looked for life and saw it was a shade;
I trod the earth, and knew it was my tomb,
And now I die, and now I was but made.
My glass is full, and now my glass is run;
And now I live, and now my life is done.

This is supposed to be the best bit of his life.

All these lines are phrased in the same way.

He might be referring to his trial, or to the story of his life.

The fallen fruit represents his death, the green leaves represent his youth.

Nearly every word in the poem has just one syllable, making it sound plain and direct.

He probably means an hourglass (he's running out of time).

Gloomy language.

The day represents life, the sun represents enjoyment of life.

This line is repeated at the end of the other two verses as well.

The repetition of "and yet" emphasises the irony of his situation — his life's over, and yet he's still young.

The lines in this verse sound like riddles.

Contrast: end of life and beginning of life.

Very foreboding language — he's convinced he's going to die.

The poem has a regular rhyme scheme.

He hasn't got any hope.

POEM DICTIONARY
elegy — a song or verse commemorating a dead person
tares — weeds
shade — old-fashioned word for a ghost

Tichborne's Elegy

Chidiock Tichborne was about to be executed when he wrote this poem. Unsurprisingly, he's not too chuffed about the idea of dying. Little did he know that he would find everlasting life, in the pages of the GCSE AQA English Literature Anthology...

You've Got To Know What Happens in the Poem

Lines 1-6 Tichborne contrasts his health and youth with the fact that he's about to die. He uses a series of metaphors to represent his situation.

Lines 7-12 Another verse on the same theme, also using metaphors.

Lines 13-18 This verse is similar to the other two, but this one mentions death directly. All three verses end with the same line, which sums up his predicament: "And now I live, and now my life is done."

Learn About the Three Types of Language

1) METAPHORICAL LANGUAGE — Tichborne uses a series of metaphors throughout the poem to make the point that he's really young and healthy, and yet his life's over anyway.
2) REPETITIVE LANGUAGE — The poem is structured in a repetitive way, e.g. each verse ends with the same line. This emphasises his main point — that he's still young, but is about to die.
3) LANGUAGE ABOUT DEATH — Death is the main theme of the poem. There's lots of miserable language and imagery about death.

Remember the Feelings and Attitudes in the Poem

1) INJUSTICE — He thinks it's unfair that he should have to die so young — he's being cut off in his prime.
2) REGRET — He feels sad that's he's got to leave life so soon.
3) BITTERNESS — There's a tiny bit of bitterness about his situation.
4) IRONY — It seems ironic to Tichborne that he's about to die even though he's young and he feels healthy.

Think About Your Feelings and Attitudes to the Poem

1) Pick 2 words or phrases that stand out to you. If none stand out, just pick 2 unusual words or phrases.
2) Write these 2 words or phrases down. Then write about how they make you feel. If they don't make you feel anything, don't worry — just make something up, as long as it's not too stupid.

EXAMPLE I find the line "And now I live, and now my life is done" very moving. The poet's clear awareness of the hopelessness of his situation is tragic. Many people in that situation might be desperately hoping for escape and freedom, but Tichborne faces his fate. I think this is brave.

Themes — death, irony and imagery...

Compare 'Tichborne's Elegy' with other poems on the same themes: death ('On my first Sonne' p.6-7 and 'Mid-Term Break' p.46-47), irony ('The Man He Killed' p.16-17 and 'Follower' p.50-51) and imagery ('Ulysses' p.26-27 and 'October' p.62-63).

Thomas Hardy

Thomas Hardy (1840-1928) was born in Dorset. He trained as an architect before becoming a very well-known novelist. He wrote classic and often controversial books like 'Jude the Obscure' and 'Far from the Madding Crowd', as well as writing poetry.

The Man He Killed

'Had he and I but met
By some old ancient inn,
We should have sat us down to wet
Right many a nipperkin!

'But ranged as infantry,
And staring face to face,
I shot at him as he at me,
And killed him in his place.

'I shot him dead because –
Because he was my foe,
Just so: my foe of course he was;
That's clear enough; although

'He thought he'd 'list, perhaps,
Off-hand like – just as I –
Was out of work – had sold his traps –
No other reason why.

'Yes; quaint and curious war is!
You shoot a fellow down
You'd treat if met where any bar is,
Or help to half-a-crown.'

- The whole poem's in speech marks — to make you imagine someone speaking out loud.
- The 1st and 3rd lines, and 2nd and 4th lines rhyme all the way through.
- Informal, friendly language — contrasts with the description of the battle in the second verse.
- Very simple, straightforward description of dramatic event.
- Repetition of 'because' shows he's stumbling to think of a reason why he killed the man.
- He reassures himself that he was right to kill the man.
- Shortened, colloquial version of "enlist" (to join the army).
- Informal language.
- The soldier imagines that the man he killed was similar to himself.
- The man he killed probably wasn't evil or nasty — just an unemployed man who joined up because he needed a job.
- This line is worded almost like it's a joke — but there's a lot of bitterness in it.
- Implies that everyone would do the same thing in a battle situation.
- Sounds more like a friend than an enemy.

POEM DICTIONARY
nipperkin — a small amount of beer or liquor
infantry — foot soldiers
foe — enemy
traps — belongings
help to — lend
half-a-crown — old British coin

The Man He Killed

In this poem, a soldier tells us about a man he killed in battle. He says that even though the man was on the opposing side, he was probably just a nice, ordinary bloke. He reckons that if he'd met the man in a pub, instead of the battlefield, they might have been friends.

You've Got To Know What Happens in the Poem

Lines 1-4 — The soldier says that he could have been friends with the other man, if they had met in an inn.

Lines 5-8 — But they met in battle, and shot at each other. The other man was killed.

Lines 9-12 — The only reason he killed the other man was that they were on different sides.

Lines 13-16 — He imagines that the man he killed may have been very similar to him — only enlisting in the army because he needed work.

Lines 17-20 — He sums up the message of the poem. He says that war is a strange business — you kill people you might have been friends with in different circumstances.

Learn About the Three Types of Language

1) COLLOQUIAL LANGUAGE — This means informal language that sounds like everyday speech. The poem is written as if the soldier is speaking to the reader.
2) MATTER-OF-FACT LANGUAGE — The soldier uses fairly matter-of-fact, down-to-earth language to describe killing the man. This detached language contrasts with the serious message behind the poem, and helps to highlight the soldier's feeling of bitterness.
3) THOUGHTFUL LANGUAGE — The soldier thinks quite deeply about what he has done. He empathises with the man he killed.

Remember the Feelings and Attitudes in the Poem

Make friends, not war.

1) IRONY — The soldier has a sense of irony about the situation — he's killed a man who he might have been friends with in different circumstances.
2) PUZZLEMENT — It troubles the soldier that the man he killed was probably quite like himself.
3) TRAGEDY — The poet's making a point about the tragedy of war.

Writing the poem from the point of view of an ordinary soldier increases the impact of the anti-war message.

Think About Your Feelings and Attitudes to the Poem

1) Pick 2 words or phrases that stand out to you. If none stand out, just pick 2 unusual words or phrases.
2) Write these 2 words or phrases down. Then write about how they make you feel. If they don't make you feel anything, don't worry — just make something up, as long as it's not too stupid.

EXAMPLE The line "Yes; quaint and curious war is!" stands out to me because it's like an emotional outburst. All the way through the poem, the narrator sounds very restrained and matter-of-fact, and then suddenly there is this bitter, sarcastic statement. I can imagine the soldier spitting the words out.

Themes — politics, irony and first person...

Compare 'The Man He Killed' with other poems about the same themes: politics ('At a Potato Digging' p.36-37 and 'The Field-Mouse' p.60-61), irony ('Tichborne's Elegy' p.14-15 and 'Follower' p.50-51) and use of the first person ('Ulysses' p.26-27 and 'Digging' p.44-45).

Key Poem

Walt Whitman

Walt Whitman (1819-1892) was an American poet born in New York. He was one of America's earliest great poets. He was also a teacher and journalist.

Patrolling Barnegat

Wild, wild the storm, and the sea high running,
Steady the roar of the gale, with incessant undertone muttering,
Shouts of demoniac laughter fitfully piercing and pealing,
Waves, air, midnight, their savagest trinity lashing,
Out in the shadows there milk-white combs careering,
On beachy slush and sand spirts of snow fierce slanting,
Where through the murk the easterly death-wind breasting,
Through cutting swirl and spray watchful and firm advancing,
(That in the distance! is that a wreck? is the red signal flaring?)
Slush and sand of the beach tireless till daylight wending,
Steadily, slowly, through hoarse roar never remitting,
Along the midnight edge by those milk-white combs careering,
A group of dim, weird forms, struggling, the night confronting,
That savage trinity warily watching.

Repeated to create a definite first impression of the storm.

An evil sound — dramatic and evil atmosphere.

The poem is one long sentence, with every line ending in "-ing" — this creates a sense of the storm happening right now, going on and on and on.

Onomatopoeic description of the sea.

Alliteration of "s" suggests the sounds of the waves of the ocean.

Makes the elements sound like an attacking force.

Sharp and dangerous, like a sword.

The patrollers fear the worst.

Sounds deep, rough and powerful.

A defensive force, protecting the land from the storm.

The people in the patrol are hard to see in the confusion and chaos of the storm.

Like sentries on look-out.

Alliteration here sounds like the waves crashing down.

The patrollers face up to the enemy (the storm).

POEM DICTIONARY
Barnegat — a bay in New Jersey, USA
incessant — never-ending
demoniac — like the devil
pealing — making a long, loud sound
trinity — three things joined together
combs — the tops of waves
careering — moving quickly
breasting — facing, standing square-on
wending — travelling
remitting — stopping

Patrolling Barnegat

Key Poem

The poet describes a fierce storm blowing at night into a bay in America.
Some people are patrolling the beach, standing up to the wild, cold wind. Brrrrrr....

You've Got To Know What Happens in the Poem

Lines 1-6 — A big storm is raging on a beach at night. Strong winds make massive waves in the sea which batter the land.

Lines 7-14 — Amid the dark and bleak night, people patrol the beach, facing up to the storm. They wonder if they can see a shipwreck in the distance (line 9).

Learn About the Two Types of Language

1) WAR-LIKE LANGUAGE — The storm is like a battleground between land and sea. The people on patrol on the beach are there to protect the land from attack.
2) SOUNDS OF THE STORM — There's lots of alliteration and onomatopoeia (words which sound like what they're describing). The poet uses these to create a sense of the sounds of the howling wind and roaring waves.

Remember the Feelings and Attitudes in the Poem

1) RESPECT — The poet respects the power of the storm.
2) ADMIRATION — He admires the bravery of the people patrolling the beach.
3) WARINESS — The people patrolling the beach are cautious (line 14).

There's a sense of dread surrounding the storm — the storm seems capable of great destruction.

Think About Your Feelings and Attitudes to the Poem

1) Pick 2 words or phrases that stand out to you. If none stand out, just pick 2 unusual words or phrases.
2) Write these 2 words or phrases down. Then write about how they make you feel. If they don't make you feel anything, don't worry — just make something up, as long as it's not too stupid.

EXAMPLE The description of the storm as a "savage trinity" fills me with fear. It sounds like a wild animal, with the three forces of the waves, air and night wildly attacking the land.

Themes — nature, danger and language effects...

Compare 'Patrolling Barnegat' with other poems about the same themes: nature ('Sonnet' p.34-35 and 'Storm on the Island' p.48-49), danger ('The Little Boy Lost'/'The Little Boy Found' p.12-13 and 'Cold Knap Lake' p.66-67) and language effects ('Perch' p.38-39 and 'Inversnaid' p.32-33).

William Shakespeare

William Shakespeare (1564-1616) was a successful playwright and poet. He was born in Stratford-upon-Avon, Warwickshire, but lived in London for most of his life. He is one of the most important figures of Elizabethan literature.

Sonnet 130

My mistress' eyes are nothing like the sun;
Coral is far more red than her lips' red.
If snow be white, why then her breasts are dun;
If hairs be wires, black wires grow on her head.
I have seen roses damasked, red and white,
But no such roses see I in her cheeks;
And in some perfumes is there more delight
Than in the breath that from my mistress reeks.
I love to hear her speak, yet well I know
That music hath a far more pleasing sound.
I grant I never saw a goddess go:
My mistress when she walks treads on the ground.
    And yet, by heaven, I think my love as rare
    As any she belied with false compare.

Shakespeare wrote over 150 sonnets. This is the 130th.

The word "nothing" changes this line from a compliment into a criticism.

These words might be found in a normal love poem.

These lines start as if they're going to be traditional compliments.

Sounds ugly and coarse. The opposite of saying someone has hair like gold.

Alternate lines rhyme for the first 12 lines.

In most love poems, the woman would be compared favourably to these things.

This is the big turning point in the poem. He does love something about her.

This woman's real — not some romantic ideal.

He's says he's never seen a goddess, so can't compare her to one. This is a bit of a dig at traditional love poetry, where women are praised unrealistically.

The sonnet ends with a rhyming couplet.

Any woman.

The last two lines are inset, making them stand out.

This exclamation shows real feeling. He does love her after all.

POEM DICTIONARY
dun — a brownish-grey colour
damasked — damask roses are a type of sweet-smelling rose, damask is a type of embroidered fabric
reeks — breathes out, smells
belied — misrepresented, shown to be false

Sonnet 130

Shakespeare spends most of the poem criticising his lover — she's not beautiful, she smells, her hair's all coarse like wire... Then he turns it all around by saying he loves her anyway. You have to hope she was the forgiving sort.

You've Got To Know What Happens in the Poem

Lines 1-4 — He makes blunt, critical statements about his mistress's looks. She doesn't match up to popular ideas of beauty in Elizabethan times, e.g. she's dark-haired, not fair.

Lines 5-12 — He lists more beautiful things (roses, music, perfume, goddesses) but then explains that she isn't like any of these either. On line 9, however, it starts to become apparent that he does like her really.

Lines 13-14 — In the final rhyming couplet, he says that he thinks his mistress is great — as good as any other woman who's been praised in love poetry.

Learn About the Three Types of Language

1) SUBVERSION OF TRADITIONAL IMAGES OF BEAUTY — Many of the lines sound like they're going to be traditional images of women's beauty. But Shakespeare goes against the reader's expectations by saying that his mistress isn't like these images — she's beautiful in a more genuine way.
2) CRITICAL LANGUAGE — He sounds pretty scathing about his mistress in the first part of the poem.
3) SONNET FORM — The poem is in traditional sonnet form. It has fourteen lines and is in iambic pentameters (see glossary). Sonnets are often used for love poetry.

Remember the Feelings and Attitudes in the Poem

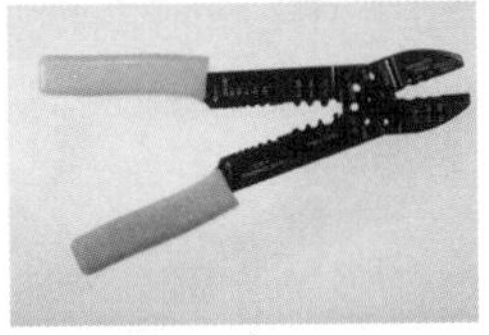

Time for a hair cut.

1) SUBVERSION — Shakespeare's having fun with this poem, turning the reader's expectations of a love poem on their head.
2) CONTEMPT — He sounds pretty insulting about his mistress's looks, voice and smell in the first part of the poem.
3) LOVE — Then at the end, the message seems to be: "I love her warts and all. I don't need to pretend she's a goddess."

Shakespeare wrote a lot of traditional love sonnets, where he would compare women to roses etc. So in a way he's taking the mick out of his own poetry in Sonnet 130.

Think About Your Feelings and Attitudes to the Poem

1) Pick 2 words or phrases that stand out to you. If none stand out, just pick 2 unusual words or phrases.
2) Write these 2 words or phrases down. Then write about how they make you feel. If they don't make you feel anything, don't worry — just make something up, as long as it's not too stupid.

EXAMPLE I really like the phrase "belied with false compare." Often when I read love poetry it does seem pretty false: no one really floats like a goddess or has a voice sweeter than music. The conclusion to this poem is surprisingly down-to-earth and realistic.

Themes — love, imagery and closing couplet...

Compare 'Sonnet 130' with other poems about the same themes: love ('Digging' p.44-45 and 'Catrin' p.52-53), imagery ('Tichborne's Elegy' p.14-15 and 'Blackberry-Picking' p.40-41) and a striking closing couplet ('The Village Schoolmaster' p.28-29 and 'Cold Knap Lake' p.66-67).

THIS IS A FLAP.
FOLD THIS PAGE OUT.

Robert Browning

Robert Browning (1812-1889) was born in Camberwell, Surrey. He read and wrote poems from an early age. He married Elizabeth Barrett, another well-known poet. He produced many collections of poems, before he died in Venice, Italy.

My Last Duchess

Ferrara

That's my last Duchess painted on the wall,
Looking as if she were alive. I call
That piece a wonder, now: Frà Pandolf's hands
Worked busily a day, and there she stands.
Will't please you sit and look at her? I said
'Frà Pandolf' by design, for never read
Strangers like you that pictured countenance,
The depth and passion of its earnest glance,
But to myself they turned (since none puts by
The curtain I have drawn for you, but I)
And seemed as they would ask me, if they durst
How such a glance came there; so, not the first
Are you to turn and ask thus. Sir, 'twas not
Her husband's presence only, called that spot
Of joy into the Duchess' cheek: perhaps
Frà Pandolf chanced to say 'Her mantle laps
'Over my lady's wrist too much,' or 'Paint
'Must never hope to reproduce the faint
'Half-flush that dies along her throat:' such stuff
Was courtesy, she thought, and cause enough
For calling up that spot of joy. She had
A heart – how shall I say? – too soon made glad,
Too easily impressed; she liked whate'er
She looked on, and her looks went everywhere.
Sir, 'twas all one! My favour at her breast,
The dropping of the daylight in the West,
The bough of cherries some officious fool
Broke in the orchard for her, the white mule

- The name of a 16th century Duke.
- Sets a sinister tone.
- Sounds like he owns the Duchess herself, not just the picture of her.
- The name of the artist.
- Sounds polite, but he's really being quite forceful here.
- The portrait shows she had strong emotions.
- He controls who looks at the painting — but he couldn't control who looked at his wife when she was alive.
- Suggests people were scared of his temper.
- Creates the impression of a question from the visitor.
- Reference to death is out of place and suspicious.
- Repeating this shows it bothers him.
- The Duke struggles to express his irritation.
- She was cheery and friendly — but the Duke means this as a criticism.
- She flirted a lot — the Duke thinks so anyway.
- He sounds like he's justifying himself — he's on the defensive.

Robert Browning

She rode with round the terrace – all and each
Would draw from her alike the approving speech,
Or blush, at least. She thanked men, – good! but thanked–
Somehow – I know not how – as if she ranked
My gift of a nine-hundred-years-old name
With anybody's gift. Who'd stoop to blame
This sort of trifling? Even had you skill
In speech – (which I have not) – to make your will
Quite clear to such a one, and say, 'Just this
'Or that in you disgusts me; here you miss,
'Or there exceed the mark' – and if she let
Herself be lessoned so, nor plainly set
Her wits to yours, forsooth and made excuse,
– E'en then would be some stooping; and I choose
Never to stoop. Oh sir, she smiled, no doubt,
Whene'er I passed her; but who passed without
Much the same smile? This grew; I gave commands;
Then all smiles stopped together. There she stands
As if alive. Will't please you to rise? We'll meet
The company below, then. I repeat,
The Count your master's known munificence
Is ample warrant that no just pretence
Of mine for dowry will be disallowed;
Though his fair daughter's self, as I avowed
At starting, is my object. Nay, we'll go
Together down, sir. Notice Neptune, though,
Taming a sea-horse, thought a rarity,
Which Claus of Innsbruck cast in bronze for me.

- The Duke's jealous — he suggests the Duchess flirted with everyone.
- He's proud of his history, his important family and the titles of "Duke" and "Duchess".
- False modesty — he clearly does like speaking.
- He says you shouldn't judge people — but it seems he couldn't help it.
- This word suggests he was more bothered about the Duchess's behaviour than he's letting on.
- He thinks spoken criticism is beneath him — suggests he found some other way of dealing with the problem.
- He sounds suspicious of her — maybe he thought she was being unfaithful.
- He doesn't explain how this happened, which makes it sound sinister.
- Shows his power — but we don't find out what the commands were.
- The Duke reminds his visitor of his low status.
- He's arranging his next marriage — his Next Duchess.
- Sounds polite, but he's definitely in charge.
- Moves onto another valuable possession as if he's said nothing unusual.

POEM DICTIONARY

countenance — face
durst — dare
mantle — cloak
bough — branch
forsooth — indeed
officious — fawning
munificence — generosity
dowry — money paid to a man by his bride's family when they marry
avowed — said
Neptune — Roman god of the sea

My Last Duchess

In this poem, a Duke is talking to a visitor about a portrait of his wife, who is now dead. He says he really likes the picture, but then he goes on about how she used to smile and have a laugh with everyone, and this annoyed him. We begin to suspect her death may have been a bit suspicious.

You've Got To Know What Happens in the Poem

Lines 1-5	The Duke points out the portrait of the Duchess to a visitor. He's very proud of it.
Lines 5-13	He says people always ask him about the passionate expression on the Duchess's face.
Lines 13-21	The Duke says the Duchess's flirty expression wasn't reserved just for him.
Lines 21-34	He says she smiled at everyone. He's annoyed that she treated him just like anyone else.
Lines 34-43	He says it would have been wrong to criticise her for her behaviour.
Lines 43-47	He acted to stop the Duchess's flirting — but, suspiciously, he doesn't say how he did this.
Lines 47-56	The Duke and his guest walk away from the painting. The Duke reveals he's planning to get married again, this time to the daughter of a Count.

Learn About the Four Types of Language

1) JEALOUS LANGUAGE — The things the Duke says about the Duchess sound quite innocent at first. But we can read hidden meanings into them which hint at the Duke's jealousy, e.g. by saying she smiled a lot, he seems to suggest that she was a flirt, and maybe unfaithful to him.
2) SINISTER LANGUAGE — The Duke sometimes says things that make him sound a bit sinister — there's a dark side to him. We begin to suspect that he might have killed the Duchess.
3) LANGUAGE ABOUT POWER — The Duke feels the need to have power and control over the Duchess. He sees her as another of his possessions, just like his expensive paintings.
4) FORMAL LANGUAGE — The Duke talks in a polite, old-fashioned way. He sometimes uses this to cover up the fact that he says some pretty nasty and suspicious things.

Remember the Feelings and Attitudes in the Poem

"The brazen hussy..."

1) PRIDE — The Duke is very proud of his possessions and his status.
2) JEALOUSY — He couldn't stand the way the Duchess treated him no better than anyone else (lines 31-34).
3) POWER — The Duke enjoys the control he has over the painting (lines 9-10). He didn't have this power over the Duchess when she was alive.

Think About Your Feelings and Attitudes to the Poem

1) Pick 2 words or phrases that stand out to you. If none stand out, just pick 2 unusual words or phrases.
2) Write these 2 words or phrases down. Then write about how they make you feel. If they don't make you feel anything, don't worry — just make something up, as long as it's not too stupid.

EXAMPLE When the Duke says "all smiles stopped together", I'm very suspicious of the Duke. His tone suggests he was satisfied with the result of his "commands". Considering the Duchess is now dead, this seems rather sinister to me.

Themes — attitudes to others, danger and first person...

Compare 'My Last Duchess' with other poems about the same themes: attitudes to others ('The Laboratory' p.30-31 and 'Baby-sitting' p.54-55), danger ('The Field-Mouse' p.60-61) and use of the first person ('The Man He Killed' p.16-17 and 'Death of a Naturalist' p.42-43).

Alfred Tennyson

Alfred Tennyson (1809-1892) was born in Lincolnshire, and later lived on the Isle of Wight and in Surrey. He studied at Trinity College, Cambridge. Tennyson was one of the great poets of the Victorian era, and was Poet Laureate from 1850 to 1892.

Alliteration — the harsh "c" sound emphasises the roughness of the eagle and his surroundings.

Strong, determined grip.

The Eagle

He clasps the crag with crookèd hands;
Close to the sun in lonely lands,
Ring'd with the azure world, he stands.

The wrinkled sea beneath him crawls;
He watches from his mountain walls,
And like a thunderbolt he falls.

The poet describes the eagle as "he", not "it".

Surrounded by a vast emptiness.

Shows how high the eagle's position is.

He waits for the right moment before diving — he's skilful.

Simile shows the eagle's incredible natural power and speed.

Personification — the eagle is described as an old man.

Far away and alone.

He seems to be waiting.

The sea appears slow and tame from his perspective.

Like a house. The eagle owns the mountain.

Contrast with the end of the first verse. The two sides of the eagle are shown — first waiting, now acting.

POEM DICTIONARY
azure — blue

The Eagle

The poet describes a magnificent eagle. That's it.

You've Got To Know What Happens in the Poem

Lines 1-3 — The eagle stands on a cliff, in front of the sun and surrounded by the big blue sky.
Lines 4-6 — The eagle patiently watches the sea, then dives into it for food, quick as a flash.

Learn About the Three Types of Language

1) PERSONIFICATION — The poet describes the eagle as if it's a person he respects — e.g. he says "him" rather that "it". The eagle is like an admirable old man.
2) ISOLATION — The eagle is alone and unique. He belongs to the sky around him, not the earth way below.
3) POWERFUL LANGUAGE — The eagle is strong and fast. He's the king of everything he sees.

The rhyming triplets and regular rhythm create an impression of the natural beauty of the scene.

Remember the Feelings and Attitudes in the Poem

"Here, fishy-fishy..."

1) RESPECT — The poet respects the magnificent strong figure of the eagle, perched on the cliff.
2) ADMIRATION — He also admires the physical speed and power of the eagle when he dives towards the sea.

Lines 1-3 show how great the eagle looks just standing there. Lines 4-6 show how good he looks in action.

Think About Your Feelings and Attitudes to the Poem

1) Pick 2 words or phrases that stand out to you. If none stand out, just pick 2 unusual words or phrases.
2) Write these 2 words or phrases down. Then write about how they make you feel. If they don't make you feel anything, don't worry — just make something up, as long as it's not too stupid.

EXAMPLE The simile "like a thunderbolt" makes me feel amazed at the eagle's speed. His dive happens in a flash, almost too quick to see, but also with great power.

Themes — nature and imagery...

Compare 'The Eagle' with other poems about the same themes: nature ('Perch' p.38-39, 'At a Potato Digging' p.36-37, 'Inversnaid' p.32-33 and 'Sonnet' p.34-35), and imagery ('Storm on the Island' p.48-49, 'Mali' p.56-57 and 'The Little Boy Lost'/'The Little Boy Found' p.12-13).

THIS IS A FLAP.
FOLD THIS PAGE OUT.

Alfred Tennyson

Ulysses

It little profits that an idle king,
By this still hearth, among these barren crags,
Matched with an agèd wife, I mete and dole
Unequal laws unto a savage race,
That hoard, and sleep, and feed, and know not me.

I cannot rest from travel: I will drink
Life to the lees: all times I have enjoyed
Greatly, have suffered greatly, both with those
That loved me, and alone; on shore, and when
Through scudding drifts the rainy Hyades
Vext the dim sea; I am become a name;
For always roaming with a hungry heart
Much have I seen and known; cities of men
And manners, climates, councils, governments,
Myself not least, but honoured of them all;
And drunk delight of battle with my peers,
Far on the ringing plains of windy Troy.
I am a part of all that I have met;
Yet all experience is an arch wherethrough
Gleams that untravelled world, whose margin fades
For ever and for ever when I move.
How dull it is to pause, to make an end,
To rust unburnished, not to shine in use!
As though to breathe were life. Life piled on life
Were all too little, and of one to me
Little remains: but every hour is saved
From that eternal silence, something more,
A bringer of new things; and vile it were
For some three suns to store and hoard myself,
And to this gray spirit yearning in desire
To follow knowledge like a sinking star,
Beyond the utmost bound of human thought.

This is my son, mine own Telemachus,
To whom I leave the sceptre and the isle –
Well-loved of me, discerning to fulfil
This labour, by slow prudence to make mild
A rugged people, and through soft degrees
Subdue them to the useful and the good.
Most blameless is he, centred in the sphere
Of common duties, decent not to fail
In offices of tenderness, and pay
Meet adoration to my household gods,
When I am gone. He works his work, I mine.

- The plodding rhythm in this verse reflects his boredom and frustration.
- Drab, down-to-earth setting.
- This sums up his attitude.
- He's determined to use up every last second of life.
- He knows he's famous.
- He's proud and confident.
- Alliteration adds to the sense of eagerness.
- Describes how warriors become intoxicated with the excitement of battle.
- The ancient city where the Trojan War was fought.
- Suggests he belongs in other places, not just his original home.
- Each adventure makes you realise how many more adventures there are out there — you never feel like you've done everything.
- He feels useless and bored when he's resting.
- Compares himself to a sword, rusting through lack of use.
- He does not have enough time left to do all the things he wants to do.
- He's desperate for new experiences.
- He wants to carry on travelling forever — his journey will never be complete.
- Descriptions of his son's duties contrast with the excitement of Ulysses's adventures.
- He's going on a voyage but also facing up to death.
- He and his son are different kinds of people.

Alfred Tennyson

There lies in the port; the vessel puffs her sail:
There gloom the dark broad seas. My mariners,
Souls that have toiled, and wrought, and thought with me –
That ever was a frolic welcome took
The thunder and the sunshine, and opposed
Free hearts, free foreheads – you and I are old;
Old age hath yet his honour and his toil;
Death closes all: but something ere the end,
Some work of noble note, may yet be done,
Not unbecoming men that strove with Gods.
The lights begin to twinkle from the rocks:
The long day wanes: the slow moon climbs: the deep
Moans round with many voices. Come, my friends,
'Tis not too late to seek a newer world.
Push off, and sitting well in order smite
The sounding furrows; for my purpose holds
To sail beyond the sunset, and the baths
Of all the western stars, until I die.
It may be that the gulfs will wash us down:
It may be we shall touch the Happy Isles,
And see the great Achilles, whom we knew.
Though much is taken, much abides; and though
We are not now that strength which in old days
Moved earth and heaven; that which we are, we are;
One equal temper of heroic hearts,
Made weak by time and fate, but strong in will
To strive, to seek, to find and not to yield.

- The seas are dark and intimidating — this seems to add to their appeal.
- He reminds his crew of their past achievements.
- He's realistic — just because he's a hero, he doesn't think he's invincible.
- He reminds his mariners that they don't have much time left in life.
- The end of the day symbolises the end of their lifetimes.
- He feels the sea is calling him away.
- Talks to the seamen as his equals.
- These phrases suggest he's talking about the afterlife.
- Another reminder that death isn't far away.
- He tells his band of men that he's united with them, to make them feel ready to set off together.
- Ulysses ends his speech with a rousing flourish, to stir his crew.

POEM DICTIONARY
Ulysses — Roman name for Odysseus, a Greek hero who fought in the Trojan War and spent 10 years travelling home
mete and dole — give out
lees — last drops
Hyades — in Greek mythology, the seven daughters of Atlas
vext — angered
unburnished — unpolished
Telemachus — son of Ulysses
sceptre — symbol of ruling power
prudence — care, caution
mariners — sailors
ere — before
strove — fought
smite — strike
furrows — trenches
Achilles — another Greek hero
abides — remains

Ulysses

This poem is about the ancient Greek hero Ulysses. He's returned from the Trojan War to rule his home island of Ithaca as King — but he feels restless. He decides he needs to spend the rest of his life having more adventures. The poem ends with a rousing speech to his crew.

You've Got To Know What Happens in the Poem

Lines 1-5	Ulysses has returned home. He feels frustrated and bored ruling his "savage" people.
Lines 6-32	He decides he has to continue his adventures right up to his dying day. He remembers his past adventures and says there's no point in just sitting about — he has to get all he can out of life.
Lines 33-43	He talks about his son, Telemachus. He says Telemachus is less adventurous, but he'll make a good ruler. Ulysses is proud of him — but he's a different kind of person from Ulysses.
Lines 44-61	Ulysses addresses his crew before they set off on their voyage. He says that he and they may be old, but they're brave and strong men who are still capable of new achievements.
Lines 62-70	Ulysses motivates his crew. He tells them that they're not as strong as they once were, and they may not come back alive, but they're brave men who will give their all.

Learn About the Four Types of Language

1) HEROIC LANGUAGE — Ulysses proudly describes his exciting adventures. He uses stirring, heroic language to fire up his crew before their next voyage.
2) IMAGERY — Ulysses creates some powerful images of his battles and adventures.
3) LANGUAGE ABOUT DEATH — He's well aware that he's old, and this makes him determined to get the most out of the time he has left. He mentions death several times, but he doesn't seem scared of dying.
4) LANGUAGE ABOUT FRUSTRATION — He feels bored and frustrated when he's not active.

Remember the Feelings and Attitudes in the Poem

1) BOREDOM — Ulysses feels bored by the thought of ruling his people at home. He seems scornful of them: "a savage race".
2) PRIDE — Ulysses is proud of his brave reputation and his great achievements in the past.
3) EXCITEMENT — He looks forward to the coming voyage and uses his own excitement to inspire his crew.

Think About Your Feelings and Attitudes to the Poem

1) Pick 2 words or phrases that stand out to you. If none stand out, just pick 2 unusual words or phrases.
2) Write these 2 words or phrases down. Then write about how they make you feel. If they don't make you feel anything, don't worry — just make something up, as long as it's not too stupid.

> **EXAMPLE** I really respect Ulysses's courage when he says "my purpose holds / To sail beyond the sunset". This line shows he is determined to continue his adventures for as long as possible, and he is not afraid of death.

Themes — death, memory and first person...

Compare 'Ulysses' with other poems about the same themes: death ('Tichborne's Elegy' p.14-15 and 'October' p.62-63), memory ('Digging' p.44-45 and 'Cold Knap Lake' p.66-67) and use of the first person ('The Song of the Old Mother' p.8-9 and 'My Last Duchess' p.22-23).

Oliver Goldsmith

Oliver Goldsmith (1728-1774) was an Irish playwright and poet. He studied at Trinity College, Dublin. He was also a translator and wrote children's books and histories.

The Village Schoolmaster

Beside yon straggling fence that skirts the way,
With blossomed furze unprofitably gay,
There, in his noisy mansion, skilled to rule,
The village master taught his little school;
A man severe he was, and stern to view,
I knew him well, and every truant knew;
Well had the boding tremblers learned to trace
The day's disasters in his morning face;
Full well they laughed, with counterfeited glee,
At all his jokes, for many a joke had he:
Full well the busy whisper, circling round,
Conveyed the dismal tidings when he frowned;
Yet he was kind, or, if severe in aught,
The love he bore to learning was in fault;
The village all declared how much he knew;
'Twas certain he could write, and cipher too;
Lands he could measure, terms and tides presage,
And even the story ran that he could gauge.
In arguing, too, the parson owned his skill,
For, even though vanquished, he could argue still;
While words of learned length and thundering sound
Amazed the gazing rustics ranged around;
And still they gazed, and still the wonder grew
That one small head could carry all he knew.

Rugged images of the countryside.

There are rhyming couplets all the way through.

Describing the school like this shows he was in charge.

It doesn't sound like he was much fun.

The children were frightened of him.

He took his bad moods out on other people.

The pupils pretended to find his jokes funny to keep him in a good mood.

Sounds like they were scared of his temper.

If he was severe, it was because he was so studious.

He had an impressive range of skills.

There were rumours about him, which implies no-one knew him all that well.

He was stubborn — he'd carry on arguing even when he was wrong.

Suggests he had a loud voice.

This could mean they were in awe of his intelligence, but the tone suggests they were just puzzled by him.

He was an outsider. The villagers didn't know what to make of him.

Fairly disrespectful way of describing the schoolmaster — the adults weren't scared of him.

He was very knowledgeable.

POEM DICTIONARY

furze — gorse bush
boding — predicting
counterfeited — faked
aught — anything
cipher — count, do arithmetic
presage — forecast
gauge — measure
rustics — people who live in the countryside

The Village Schoolmaster

This poem is about the old schoolmaster of a village school. He was a rather strange bloke — he was bad-tempered and a bit frightening, but also very intelligent and skilful. Although the poet doesn't say it outright, it seems that the people in the village thought he was a bit of an oddball.

You've Got To Know What Happens in the Poem

Lines 1-12 — The poet points out a place in the countryside where a village school was. Then we hear about how strict the schoolmaster was — he was often in a bad mood and the pupils were scared of him.

Lines 13-24 — Then the poet says how clever the schoolmaster was. He had loads of different skills. The villagers were amazed by how much he knew — although they didn't seem to like him very much.

Learn About the Three Types of Language

1) INTIMIDATING LANGUAGE — The way the schoolmaster looked and acted makes him seem scary and unpleasant. The children were afraid of his temper, and laughed at his rubbish jokes to avoid getting on the wrong side of him.
2) LANGUAGE ABOUT EDUCATION — The schoolmaster had all sorts of skills and knowledge. The villagers were amazed at how much he knew.
3) MYSTERY — He was an outsider and a loner. The people in the village didn't know much about him, and seemed to think he was a bit odd, rather than respecting him.

Remember the Feelings and Attitudes in the Poem

"Today, children, you're going to learn about how great I am."

1) FEAR — The children were scared of the schoolmaster.
2) FASCINATION — The villagers were fascinated by the schoolmaster, but they didn't respect him very much (lines 23-24).
3) MOCKERY — The poet seems to mock the school master — he creates an impression of him being a pompous show-off (although he doesn't openly say this).

Think About Your Feelings and Attitudes to the Poem

1) Pick 2 words or phrases that stand out to you. If none stand out, just pick 2 unusual words or phrases.
2) Write these 2 words or phrases down. Then write about how they make you feel. If they don't make you feel anything, don't worry — just make something up, as long as it's not too stupid.

EXAMPLE The description of the schoolmaster as having "The day's disasters in his morning face" makes him sound scary and intimidating. I wouldn't want to have him as my headteacher.

Themes — memory, attitudes to others, characters...

Compare 'The Village Schoolmaster' with other poems about the same themes: memory ('Blackberry-Picking' p.40-41 and 'Follower' p.50-51), attitudes to others ('My Last Duchess' p.22-23 and 'Baby-sitting' p.54-55) and characters ('The Song of the Old Mother' p.8-9 and 'Catrin' p.52-53).

THIS IS A FLAP. FOLD THIS PAGE OUT.

Robert Browning

The Laboratory

ANCIEN RÉGIME

> This tells us that the poem is set in France, in the days when they had a monarchy.

I

Now that I, tying thy glass mask tightly,
May gaze thro' these faint smokes curling whitely,
As thou pliest thy trade in this devil's-smithy—
Which is the poison to poison her, prithee?

> She wears a mask for safety.

> She knows what she's doing is evil.

II

He is with her, and they know that I know
Where they are, what they do: they believe my tears flow
While they laugh, laugh at me, at me fled to the drear
Empty church, to pray God in, for them! —I am here.

> She's paranoid that she's a laughing stock — this makes her more determined to get revenge.

> The whole poem is in rhyming couplets.

III

Grind away, moisten and mash up thy paste,
Pound at thy powder,—I am not in haste!
Better sit thus, and observe thy strange things,
Than go where men wait me and dance at the King's.

> The way she describes making the poison shows her violent feelings — she'd like to do these things to her rival.

> Their lives are based around the Royal Court.

IV

That in the mortar—you call it a gum?
Ah, the brave tree whence such gold oozings come!
And yonder soft phial, the exquisite blue,
Sure to taste sweetly,—is that poison too?

> She wants to know how the poison is made, and where the ingredients come from.

> The poison is precious to her.

> The colour of the poison is beautiful to her.

V

Had I but all of them, thee and thy treasures,
What a wild crowd of invisible pleasures!
To carry pure death in an earring, a casket,
A signet, a fan-mount, a filigree basket!

> There's no doubt about what she wants to happen.

> The potions are rare and valuable.

> She gets carried away with excitement, listing all the things she can think of that could hold poison.

VI

Soon, at the King's, a mere lozenge to give,
And Pauline should have just thirty minutes to live!
But to light a pastile, and Elise, with her head
And her breast and her arms and her hands, should drop dead!

> There's a dark humour here — usually people would use these to make things better.

> The idea of killing excites her.

Robert Browning

VII

Quick—is it finished? The colour's too grim!
Why not soft like the phial's, enticing and dim?
Let it brighten her drink, let her turn it and stir,
And try it and taste, ere she fix and prefer!

> She has the whole plan worked out, down to the smallest details.

VIII

What a drop! She's not little, no minion like me!
That's why she ensnared him: this never will free
The soul from those masculine eyes,—say, 'no!'
That to pulse's magnificent come-and-go.

> She's worried there's not enough poison.

> She says her lover's mistress trapped him. Maybe she thinks this justifies her own violence.

> Respectful way of describing life — but she wants to end it.

IX

For only last night, as they whispered, I brought
My own eyes to bear on her so, that I thought
Could I keep them one half minute fixed, she would fall
Shrivelled; she fell not; yet this does it all!

> Graphic description of death.

X

Not that I bid you spare her the pain;
Let death be felt and the proof remain:
Brand, burn up, bite into its grace—
He is sure to remember her dying face!

> She wants the mistress to suffer — she wants absolute revenge.

> She takes pleasure in the cruelty of what she's doing.

XI

Is it done? Take my mask off! Nay, be not morose;
It kills her, and this prevents seeing it close:
The delicate droplet, my whole fortune's fee!
If it hurts her, beside, can it ever hurt me?

> She's so keen to see the poison, she risks removing her protective mask.

> The poison is her most prized possession, possibly her only one.

XII

Now, take all my jewels, gorge gold to your fill,
You may kiss me, old man, on my mouth if you will!
But brush this dust off me, lest horror it brings
Ere I know it—next moment I dance at the King's!

> She spends everything she has on the poison.

> She's delighted that the poison is ready.

POEM DICTIONARY

thy — your
thou — you
pliest — carry out
smithy — workshop
prithee — please
mortar — a small bowl
whence — from where
yonder — over there
phial — a small bottle
thee — you
signet — a seal on a ring
filigree — delicate ornamental metal
lozenge — a tablet or pill
pastile — a substance burnt to clean the air
ere — before
minion — a small, weak person

The Laboratory

This poem's set in France back in the days when they had a monarchy. A rich woman is buying some poison so that she can kill a woman who is having an affair with her lover/husband (we never find out who the man is). Seems a trifle extreme...

You've Got To Know What Happens in the Poem

Lines 1-4	The woman talks to the chemist while he mixes the poison in his workshop.
Lines 5-8	Her lover is with another woman and they think she's at church crying — but she's not.
Lines 9-20	She watches the chemist and says how lovely the poisons look. She wants all of them.
Lines 21-24	She plans to poison two other women called Pauline and Elise at the King's Court.
Lines 25-28	She tells the chemist to make the poison brighter, to make her lover's mistress drink it.
Lines 29-32	She says there's not enough poison to kill the mistress — she's too big and strong.
Lines 33-40	Last night, she felt she could kill the mistress by looking at her. She wants her to die painfully.
Lines 41-48	She's so grateful to the chemist she offers to kiss him. Now she's off to use the poison.

Learn About the Three Types of Language

1) VIOLENT LANGUAGE — She's absolutely merciless about taking her revenge. She wants the mistress's death to be horrible and painful, and violent thoughts are never far from her mind.
2) IMAGERY — For all her nastiness, she can be quite eloquent with her descriptions.
3) OBSESSIVE LANGUAGE — She gives up all her wealth and possessions for the poison — nothing else matters to her. She gets very excited when she thinks about revenge.

Remember the Feelings and Attitudes in the Poem

Ice with your poison, I mean drink?

1) OBSESSION — She's obsessed with the thought of getting revenge.
2) SINGLE-MINDEDNESS — revenge is all that matters to her.
3) IMMORALITY — She knows what she's doing is wrong, but she doesn't care.

She wants to kill the mistress just to get revenge on her lover for being unfaithful — pretty twisted really.

Think About Your Feelings and Attitudes to the Poem

1) Pick 2 words or phrases that stand out to you. If none stand out, just pick 2 unusual words or phrases.
2) Write these 2 words or phrases down. Then write about how they make you feel. If they don't make you feel anything, don't worry — just make something up, as long as it's not too stupid.

EXAMPLE I am horrified by the line "He is sure to remember her dying face!". She wants her lover to see his mistress when she dies, which is a very sick way of getting revenge on him.

Themes — death, attitude towards others, strong emotions...

Compare 'The Laboratory' with other poems about the same themes: death ('The Man He Killed' p.16-17 and 'October' p.62-63), attitude towards others ('My Last Duchess' p.22-23 and 'Baby-sitting' p.54-55) and strong emotions ('The Affliction of Margaret' p.10-11).

Gerard Manley Hopkins

Gerard Manley Hopkins (1844-1889) was born in Stratford, Essex. He studied Classics at Balliol College, Oxford, and was a famous Victorian poet. He became a Jesuit priest and concentrated on teaching and preaching for several years, before resuming his writing.

Inversnaid

This darksome burn, horseback brown,
His rollrock highroad roaring down,
In coop and in comb the fleece of his foam
Flutes and low to the lake falls home.

A windpuff-bonnet of fawn-froth
Turns and twindles over the broth
Of a pool so pitchblack, fell-frowning,
It rounds and rounds Despair to drowning.

Degged with dew, dappled with dew
Are the groins of the braes that the brook treads through,
Wiry heathpacks, flitches of fern,
And the beadbonny ash that sits over the burn.

What would the world be, once bereft
Of wet and of wildness? Let them be left,
O let them be left, wildness and wet;
Long live the weeds and the wilderness yet.

Repetition of how dark the stream is.

Alliteration of "c" sounds makes the stream sound rough.

The water sounds melodic.

Continual motion, like a whirlpool.

Alliteration and repetition shows that there's dew all around.

The tree is motionless but alive.

Uses a rhetorical question to appeal to the reader's emotions.

Alliteration of "r" sounds reminds us of the roar of water.

The bubbles of the stream are described like they're a person's or animal's hair.

The froth is like a hat on the water.

Hostile and unwelcoming.

The stream moves like a person walking.

Repetition creates a passionate, emotional feel.

"W" sounds are repeated throughout this verse.

POEM DICTIONARY
burn — stream
coop — an enclosed area
comb — the top of a wave
fawn — light greyish-brown colour
fell — fiercely
degged — sprinkled
braes — hills
flitches — cuttings
bereft — deprived

Inversnaid

This poem is about a burn (stream) flowing through a rugged, unspoilt area of Scotland. The area is wild and beautiful, and the poet wants it to stay that way. Don't we all, Gerard...

You've Got To Know What Happens in the Poem

- Lines 1-4 — A dark-coloured stream flows down into a lake.
- Lines 5-8 — The stream sounds dark and angry.
- Lines 9-12 — There's dew on the hills, some wild plants, and an ash tree by the river.
- Lines 13-16 — The poet says we should leave beautiful places like this as they are.

Learn About the Three Types of Language

1) SOUND EFFECTS — There's loads of alliteration to create the effect of the fast flow of water. There's also plenty of rhyming, assonance and onomatopoeia (see glossary, p.92) to help us feel like we can really hear the sounds of the country. These effects add to the rugged, natural feel.
2) PERSONIFICATION — The burn is described as if it's a person. This allows the poet to make it sound angry and fierce, and also strong and admirable.
3) EMOTIONAL LANGUAGE — The poet feels passionately that places like this should be left alone. He seems to be worried that the growth of towns and cities means there are fewer and fewer unspoilt areas of countryside.

Remember the Feelings and Attitudes in the Poem

Something's not right...

1) DANGER — The stream seems fierce and dangerous.
2) BEAUTY — The whole area is beautiful, rugged and unspoilt.
3) PRESERVATION — The poet wants this place to stay as it is. He believes it would be terrible if beautiful, natural places like this didn't exist anymore.

Think About Your Feelings and Attitudes to the Poem

1) Pick 2 words or phrases that stand out to you. If none stand out, just pick 2 unusual words or phrases.
2) Write these 2 words or phrases down. Then write about how they make you feel. If they don't make you feel anything, don't worry — just make something up, as long as it's not too stupid.

EXAMPLE When the poet asks "What would the world be, once bereft / Of wet and wildness?", it makes me sad. I live in a city, a long way from anywhere like the place the poet describes, and I think it is a pity that so many people grow up without knowing places like this.

Themes — nature, strong emotions, language effects...

Compare 'Inversnaid' with other poems about the same themes: nature ('Perch' p.38-39 and 'At a Potato Digging' p.36-37), strong emotions ('On my first Sonne' p.6-7 and 'Blackberry-Picking' p.40-41) and language effects ('Patrolling Bargenat' p.18-19 and 'Perch' p.38-39).

Key Poem

John Clare

John Clare (1793-1864) was the son of a Northampton labourer. He left school at 11 and educated himself after that. For most of his life he lived in rural Northamptonshire. He is famous for writing poems about life in the country, although he also wrote about politics, the environment, corruption and poverty.

Sonnet

I love to see the summer beaming forth
And white wool sack clouds sailing to the north
I love to see the wild flowers come again
And Mare blobs stain with gold the meadow drain
And water lilies whiten on the floods
Where reed clumps rustle like a wind shook wood
Where from her hiding place the Moor Hen pushes
And seeks her flag nest floating in bull rushes
I like the willow leaning half way o'er
The clear deep lake to stand upon its shore
I love the hay grass when the flower head swings
To summer winds and insects happy wings
That sport about the meadow the bright day
And see bright beetles in the clear lake play

Repetition emphasises his feelings.

The colour of wool suggests the purity and cleanliness of the soft, fluffy clouds.

Yellow and white enforce the brightness of early summer.

Trees around the lake make it seem alive and healthy.

Natural and unspoilt.

The insects are playful and fun-loving.

Alliteration enforces the idea of brightness.

The whole scene is shining brightly.

Using "gold" instead of yellow is an idealistic way of seeing it.

Suggests there's a light, pleasant breeze.

Rhyming couplets throughout the poem.

Gentle movement.

Brightness continues to the end of the poem.

The poem finishes on a light-hearted, carefree note.

POEM DICTIONARY

sonnet — a poem with 14 lines
Mare blobs — buttercups
Moor Hen — a bird that lives on ponds
flag — type of leaf
bull rushes — plants that grow in ponds
o'er — over

Sonnet

Key Poem

This is a good old-fashioned poem about how lovely summer in the countryside is. It's a really idealistic poem — the poet talks about all the best things in summer, like pretty flowers, trees and meadows (and ignores things like hayfever and another dull series of Big Brother).

You've Got To Know What Happens in the Poem

Lines 1-4 The poet describes how much he likes the lovely summer, with the lovely clouds floating over the lovely flowers in the lovely meadow.

Lines 5-10 Lilies and reeds grow in the lake. A bird swims across the water. The poet says how great the willow trees on the banks are.

Lines 11-14 He says he loves the way the grass and flowers blow in the wind, and cheery little insects skip about on the surface of the lake.

Learn About the Two Types of Language

1) VISUAL LANGUAGE — Nature is in full bloom. The sun is out, the fields are golden — even the beetles are bright...
2) PEACEFULNESS — The countryside is quiet and calm. The flowers are swaying in the gentle breeze. The insects are just messing round and not stinging anyone. It's a very idealistic poem.

There's no punctuation in the poem. This helps the poet to create one big image, made up of all the different things he describes.

Remember the Feelings and Attitudes in the Poem

Ah, the glorious British summer of 2004.

1) LOVE — He loves the summer and the natural scenery.
2) TRANQUILLITY — He feels relaxed and at peace.
3) HAPPINESS — Overall, he's just dead happy that it's summer and he's in the countryside. Bless.

Think About Your Feelings and Attitudes to the Poem

1) Pick 2 words or phrases that stand out to you. If none stand out, just pick 2 unusual words or phrases.
2) Write these 2 words or phrases down. Then write about how they make you feel. If they don't make you feel anything, don't worry — just make something up, as long as it's not too stupid.

EXAMPLE The phrase "summer beaming forth" reminds me of the long summer holidays when I was really young. The whole world seemed to be bright and blooming, and this poem brings back the happy, relaxed feelings of that time for me.

Themes — nature, love, imagery...

Compare 'Sonnet' with other poems about the same themes: nature ('Blackberry-Picking' p.40-41 and 'October' p.62-63), love ('Mali' p.56-57) and imagery ('Patrolling Barnegat' p.18-19, 'Inversnaid' p.32-33 and 'Perch' p.38-39).

THIS IS A FLAP. FOLD THIS PAGE OUT.

Key Poem

At a Potato Digging

Seamus Heaney was born in 1939 in County Derry, Northern Ireland, the eldest of 9 children. He grew up on his father's farm, where traditional farming methods were still used. He went to boarding school in the city of Derry, and then on to university in Belfast. His first book of poems was published in 1965. In 1995, he was awarded the Nobel prize for literature. He is married with 3 children, and divides his time between Ireland and Harvard University in the USA, where he is a professor.

At a Potato Digging

I

A mechanical digger wrecks the drill,
Spins up a dark shower of roots and mould.
Labourers swarm behind, stoop to fill
Wicker creels. Fingers go dead in the cold.

This shows that section I of the poem is set in the present.

"roots" has a double-meaning — plant roots and personal history.

The workers are compared to birds.

There are already references to death.

Like crows attacking crow-black fields, they stretch
A higgledy line from hedge to headland;
Some pairs keep breaking ragged ranks to fetch
A full creel to the pit and straighten, stand

Alliteration gives the impression of the potato diggers all working together.

Because this phrase is broken up by the end of the stanza, the poem pauses, just like the people digging.

Tall for a moment but soon stumble back
To fish a new load from the crumbled surf.
Heads bow, trunks bend, hands fumble towards the black
Mother. Processional stooping through the turf

There's a lot of religious imagery here — the diggers are worshipping the earth.

Recurs mindlessly as autumn. Centuries
Of fear and homage to the famine god
Toughen the muscles behind their humbled knees,
Make a seasonal altar of the sod.

More religious imagery. Religion, especially Catholicism, has traditionally been an important part of Irish culture.

II

Flint-white, purple. They lie scattered
like inflated pebbles. Native
to the black hutch of clay
where the halved seed shot and clotted
these knobbed and slit-eyed tubers seem
the petrified hearts of drills. Split
by the spade, they show white as cream.

These descriptions of the potatoes make them sound solid and healthy.

Alliteration.

Simile.

Good smells exude from crumbled earth.
The rough bark of humus erupts
knots of potatoes (a clean birth)
whose solid feel, whose wet inside
promises taste of ground and root.
To be piled in pits; live skulls, blind-eyed.

It's as if the potatoes are being born to Mother Earth.

This describes the potatoes — they have eyes, but don't see.

At a Potato Digging

III

Live skulls, blind-eyed, balanced on
wild higgledy skeletons
scoured the land in 'forty-five,
wolfed the blighted root and died.

This phrase is repeated from line 29, but now it's referring to real skulls.

This word is repeated from line 6, where it was used for the modern workers.

There's a direct reference to what happened during the potato famine here, so you know this section is about the past.

The new potato, sound as stone,
putrefied when it had lain
three days in the long clay pit.
Millions rotted along with it.

This could be talking about potatoes, or about the famine victims.

Mouths tightened in, eyes died hard,
faces chilled to a plucked bird.
In a million wicker huts
beaks of famine snipped at guts.

This is a contrast to the people looking like birds in lines 5 and 39 — now the famine is like a bird pecking at their stomachs (or perhaps birds are eating the unburied corpses).

In this section the 1st and 2nd lines rhyme, and so do the 3rd and 4th lines. There are also quite a lot of half-rhymes.

A people hungering from birth,
grubbing, like plants, in the bitch earth,
were grafted with a great sorrow.
Hope rotted like a marrow.

Here the poet compares people to plants, and hope to a vegetable.

Stinking potatoes fouled the land,
pits turned pus into filthy mounds:
and where potato diggers are
you still smell the running sore.

This language gives you a pretty horrible picture of the rotting potatoes.

The repeated 'p' and 's' make the descriptions of rotting potatoes sound more disgusting.

This is in the present tense, and links part III in the past to the other parts which are in the present.

IV

Under a gay flotilla of gulls
The rhythm deadens, the workers stop.
Brown bread and tea in bright canfuls
Are served for lunch. Dead-beat, they flop

In sections I and IV the 1st and 3rd lines rhyme, and so do the 2nd and 4th. There are more full rhymes in these sections.

The bright imagery in this stanza contrasts with section III.

Down in the ditch and take their fill,
Thankfully breaking timeless fasts;
Then, stretched on the faithless ground, spill
Libations of cold tea, scatter crumbs.

This is religious imagery — people often fast for religious reasons.

The word 'dead' is a reminder of the past famine.

The Earth hasn't been faithful to the people because it turned against them during the famine.

POEM DICTIONARY

wicker creels — baskets made from woven sticks
higgledy — uneven, messed up
Mother — Mother Earth (the land)
homage — honour, worship
inflated — grown larger
tubers — roots
humus — part of the soil
blighted — diseased
putrefied — decayed
grafted — join one plant to another
sore — wound
flotilla — a small fleet
dead-beat — tired-out, exhausted
fast — period of not eating anything
libation — pouring liquid out as part of a sacrifice to a god

At a Potato Digging

Key Poem

Ireland was hit by a Potato Famine in 1845 — a disease called potato blight made the potatoes rot, and thousands of people died from hunger. This poem moves between a modern-day potato harvest, and the Potato Famine.

You've Got To Know What Happens in the Poem

Section I	A description of present day digging and collecting of potatoes.
Section II	A description of the potatoes themselves.
Section III	The Potato Famine — the potato blight and the starving people.
Section IV	A more positive picture of the modern-day workers, having a break.

Learn About the Four Types of Language

1) IMAGERY — There's loads of descriptive language for you to get your teeth into here — like the good potatoes being described as pebbles (line 18) and stone (line 34), making them sound solid and healthy, in contrast to the rotted ones during the famine.
2) PAST AND PRESENT — The poet uses a different rhyme scheme for the sections about the present and the past. The poet also uses different tenses to show you where the poem moves between the past and the present.
3) ALLITERATION — There's a lot of alliteration in this poem, e.g. the repeated letters in the second stanza emphasise how the potato diggers are all working together doing a repetitive job.
4) RELIGIOUS LANGUAGE — Heaney makes a lot of religious references in this poem, and refers to Mother Earth and the famine god (lines 12 and 14). It's as if he's suggesting that the people worship the soil.

Remember the Feelings and Attitudes in the Poem

1) IRISH CULTURE — The poet sees strong links between potatoes and the Irish, past and present — he feels it's part of their culture.
2) HORROR OF FAMINE — He experiences horror, anger and disgust at the effects of famine, and sees reminders of it in the present.
3) RESILIENCE — He appreciates the Irish resilience, as they continue to rely on the potato crop, and to work hard harvesting it.

Think About Your Feelings and Attitudes to the Poem

1) Pick 2 words or phrases that stand out to you. If none stand out, just pick 2 unusual words or phrases.
2) Write these 2 words or phrases down. Then write about how they make you feel. If they don't make you feel anything, don't worry — just make something up, as long as it's not too stupid.

EXAMPLE The words "putrefied" and "rotted" on lines 35 and 37 make me feel unsettled. They could apply both to the potatoes and to the rotting corpses of the famine victims. The imagery of death and decay in this poem helps me to imagine what the Potato Famine might have been like.

Themes — death, politics and language effects...

Compare 'At a Potato Digging' with other poems about the same themes: death ('On the Train' p.64-65 and 'The Laboratory' p.30-31), politics ('A Difficult Birth, Easter 1998' p.58-59 and 'The Field-Mouse' p.60-61) and language effects ('Perch' p.38-39 and 'Inversnaid' p.32-33).

Perch

Play on words — there are 2 meanings of "perch" on the same line.

The trees cast shadows on the water.

The way the fish flicker about, as well as reminding us of the waves in the water.

Perch

Perch on their water-perch hung in the clear Bann River
Near the clay bank in alder-dapple and waver,

Perch we called 'grunts', little flood-slubs, runty and ready,
I saw and I see in the river's glorified body

That is passable through, but they're bluntly holding the pass,
Under the water-roof, over the bottom, adoze,

Guzzling the current, against it, all muscle and slur
In the finland of perch, the fenland of alder, on air

That is water, on carpets of Bann stream, on hold
In the everything flows and steady go of the world.

Seeing the fish now makes the poet remember watching them in the past.

Alliteration and assonance reinforce the idea that the fish look drab and unremarkable.

The river is big and impressive.

The fish stubbornly resist the flow of the river.

Compound word makes the river seem like a house.

Assonance links the blurred movement of the fish with the smooth, air-like rush of water.

The name of a country, but here it means a world full of fishes' fins.

Assonance links these 2 words.

Suggests stillness — nothing changes between past and present.

This continues the sentence on the previous line, connecting air and water.

Strange grammar creates the idea of continual, flowing movement.

POEM DICTIONARY
alder — type of tree
dapple — spotted mark
fen — low-lying land (often marsh-land)

Perch

The poet remembers watching perch (a type of fish) swimming in a river when he was younger, and uses this memory to talk about how the world is always moving — but maybe never actually changing. Seamus, they're just fish...

You've Got To Know What Happens in the Poem

Lines 1-2 The perch are described, swimming in the Bann River.

Lines 3-4 The poet remembers how when he was younger, he and others called the perch "grunts". He still sees them now as he saw them in the past.

Lines 5-8 The perch swim against the current.

Lines 9-10 He compares the sight of the fish to comings and goings of the world in general.

Learn About the Three Types of Language

1) AMBIGUOUS WORDS — Some words are ambiguous — they have more than one meaning, or change their meaning between different parts of the poem. This keeps the reader guessing about what the poem will describe next.
2) SOUND EFFECTS — There's a lot of assonance, especially between words at the ends of different lines. This links the ideas of different lines together. Alliteration also helps to build up an ongoing effect of the sounds of the river.
3) PAST and PRESENT — It's sometimes unclear whether what the poet describes is happening now or in the past. The past and present seem to merge together in the poet's mind.

Remember the Feelings and Attitudes in the Poem

"Who are you calling 'runty'?"

1) FAMILIARITY — Heaney sees the fish as ordinary on the face of it (line 3).
2) ADMIRATION — He's impressed by the sight of the river (line 4). His descriptions suggest he sees the place as almost magical.
3) PHILOSOPHY — His memories from when he was younger make him think of how the world keeps on moving all the time, even if we're not aware of it.

Think About Your Feelings and Attitudes to the Poem

1) Pick 2 words or phrases that stand out to you. If none stand out, just pick 2 unusual words or phrases.
2) Write these 2 words or phrases down. Then write about how they make you feel. If they don't make you feel anything, don't worry — just make something up, as long as it's not too stupid.

EXAMPLE I find the description of "the river's glorified body" very effective because it makes the river sound like a huge, living being. This phrase reminds me of the River Tweed near my home, which sometimes looks like a body stretching out through the valleys.

Themes — nature, memory and language effects...

Compare 'Perch' with other poems about the same themes: nature ('Death of a Naturalist' p.42-43 and 'Sonnet' p.34-35), memory ('Blackberry Picking' p.40-41 and 'Cold Knap Lake' p.66-67) and language effects, ('Inversnaid' p.32-33 and 'The Eagle' p.24-25).

Blackberry-Picking

Blackberry-Picking

For Philip Hobsbaum

Late August, given heavy rain and sun
For a full week, the blackberries would ripen.
At first, just one, a glossy purple clot
Among others, red, green, hard as a knot.
You ate that first one and its flesh was sweet
Like thickened wine: summer's blood was in it
Leaving stains upon the tongue and lust for
Picking. Then red ones inked up and that hunger
Sent us out with milk-cans, pea-tins, jam-pots
Where briars scratched and wet grass bleached our boots.
Round hayfields, cornfields and potato-drills
We trekked and picked until the cans were full,
Until the tinkling bottom had been covered
With green ones, and on top big dark blobs burned
Like a plate of eyes. Our hands were peppered
With thorn pricks, our palms sticky as Bluebeard's.

We hoarded the fresh berries in the byre.
But when the bath was filled we found a fur,
A rat-grey fungus, glutting on our cache.
The juice was stinking too. Once off the bush
The fruit fermented, the sweet flesh would turn sour.
I always felt like crying. It wasn't fair
That all the lovely canfuls smelt of rot.
Each year I hoped they'd keep, knew they would not.

The start of the poem sounds like an adult talking — it sounds reasoned and calm.

He talks directly to the reader, to get them involved in the story.

These words make the blackberry sound sticky and rich, like blood.

Strong, intense flavour.

Adult word. The berries create an intense desire for more — it's almost an addiction.

They were so desperate to collect them that they'd use anything.

Juicy and colourful.

They didn't mind getting wet and dirty — they just wanted the berries.

The sounds of these words enhance the sense of the thickness and vivid colour of the berries.

This simile makes the berries sound grotesque.

As if they've done something wrong. The juice round their mouths might look like a blue beard too.

As if they're hiding a secret treasure.

Sounds like the fungus has stolen their food.

It's gone from one extreme to the other — delicious to disgusting.

The poet speaks in a child's voice here.

This could be a metaphor for learning that things that at first seem great often turn out bad.

He gradually realised the sad truth as he grew up.

POEM DICTIONARY
briar — a thorny plant
Bluebeard — a villain in folk stories who murders his wives
byre — a shelter for cows
cache — a hidden store

Blackberry-Picking

The poet remembers picking blackberries when he was a kid. He loved them, and picked loads — but they always went sour pretty quickly. This seems to represent growing up, and learning to accept that sometimes things turn out bad and there's nothing you can do about it.

You've Got To Know What Happens in the Poem

Lines 1-4	The poet describes picking blackberries in summer, when the first few became ripe.
Lines 5-8	The blackberries tasted delicious.
Lines 8-16	He and some others collected loads of blackberries, keeping them in cans, pots and tins.
Lines 17-21	They stored the blackberries in the shed, but they quickly went rotten.
Lines 22-24	It really upset him that the blackberries always went bad.

Learn About the Three Types of Language

1) SENSORY LANGUAGE — The taste, smell and sight of the blackberries is really intense. Strong descriptive words let the reader imagine what the berries are like.
2) CHANGING TONE OF VOICE — The poet is remembering a childhood experience. At the start of the poem, he writes in his adult voice, but at times he lapses into a more childish tone, especially towards the end of the poem. This enables us to see what happens from a child's point of view.
3) METAPHORICAL LANGUAGE — The blackberries are like a hidden treasure. When they go rotten, it's like they've been stolen. The rotten fruit reminds us that good things in life often turn bad.

Remember the Feelings and Attitudes in the Poem

Mmmmmm, blackberries...

1) DESIRE — There's an intense desire to eat the blackberries.
2) DISAPPOINTMENT — As a child, the poet was really upset and angry when the berries went rotten.
3) REGRET — The poet has a tone of regret at the realisation that there's nothing he can do to stop the berries, and other nice things, going bad.

Overall, the tone is fairly calm and reflective — but the intense feelings the poet felt as a child are never far away.

Think About Your Feelings and Attitudes to the Poem

1) Pick 2 words or phrases that stand out to you. If none stand out, just pick 2 unusual words or phrases.
2) Write these 2 words or phrases down. Then write about how they make you feel. If they don't make you feel anything, don't worry — just make something up, as long as it's not too stupid.

EXAMPLE The phrase "a rat-grey fungus, glutting on our cache" makes me feel really sorry for the poet. It must have seemed to him, as a child, that some horrible monster had broken in and eaten up his delicious treasure.

Themes — nature, getting older and imagery...

Compare 'Blackberry-Picking' with other poems about the same themes: nature ('Sonnet' p.34-35, 'Inversnaid' p.32-33), getting older ('Follower' p.50-51, 'Mid-Term Break' p.46-47), and imagery ('Mali' p.56-57, 'The Field-Mouse' p.60-61 and 'Patrolling Barnegat' p.18-19).

Key Poem

Death of a Naturalist

Death of a Naturalist

All the year the flax-dam festered in the heart
Of the townland; green and heavy headed
Flax had rotted there, weighted down by huge sods.
Daily it sweltered in the punishing sun.
Bubbles gargled delicately, bluebottles
Wove a strong gauze of sound around the smell.
There were dragon-flies, spotted butterflies,
But best of all was the warm thick slobber
Of frogspawn that grew like clotted water
In the shade of the banks. Here, every spring
I would fill jampotfuls of the jellied
Specks to range on window-sills at home,
On shelves at school, and wait and watch until
The fattening dots burst into nimble-
Swimming tadpoles. Miss Walls would tell us how
The daddy frog was called a bullfrog
And how he croaked and how the mammy frog
Laid hundreds of little eggs and this was
Frogspawn. You could tell the weather by frogs too
For they were yellow in the sun and brown
In rain.

Then one hot day when fields were rank
With cowdung in the grass the angry frogs
Invaded the flax-dam; I ducked through hedges
To a coarse croaking that I had not heard
Before. The air was thick with a bass chorus.
Right down the dam gross-bellied frogs were cocked
On sods; their loose necks pulsed like snails. Some hopped:
The slap and plop were obscene threats. Some sat
Poised like mud grenades, their blunt heads farting.
I sickened, turned, and ran. The great slime kings
Were gathered there for vengeance and I knew
That if I dipped my hand the spawn would clutch it.

Sets the unpleasant atmosphere.

Sense of 'heaviness', like a hot lazy summer's day.

Alliteration creates more atmosphere.

Assonance makes these words stronger and more important.

Alliteration creates more atmosphere.

Here's that thickness and heaviness again.

First time it's about the poet, not the dam.

Lighter word shows his excitement.

Childish words because he's talking about when he was an infant.

These words are like the ones in lines 1-10. It's hot and sticky again.

Military word.

Military word.

Disgusting images — suggest foulness.

Alliteration strengthens the words and the atmosphere created.

Military word.

This is a simile.

Onomatopoeia strengthens the atmosphere.

Military word.

This is a metaphor.

These images show the boy's fear.

POEM DICTIONARY

flax — plant with blue flowers that is usually grown for thread for cloth, and for its seed (flaxseed).

sods — piece of grass-covered soil (a piece of turf).

Death of a Naturalist

Key Poem

In this one, the poet (still that Irish fella Seamus Heaney) writes about frogs and frogspawn. It's about when his feelings towards them changed. At first he was fascinated by them. But later the sight of grown frogs at a dam where he used to play made him scared.

You've Got To Know What Happens in the Poem

Lines 1-10	The flax-dam is described (a dam in a river, made of the plant, flax).
Lines 11-15	These talk about the poet's enthusiasm and excitement for the frogs and the dam.
Lines 15-21	These are about the infant teacher's fairy-story approach to it all.
Line 21	This is where the change happens. The change is emphasised by the words "In rain" being on their own, and a new stanza beginning.
Lines 22-30	These describe the poet discovering the scary adult frogs.
Lines 31-33	These describe the poet's disgust and fear.

Learn About the Three Types of Language

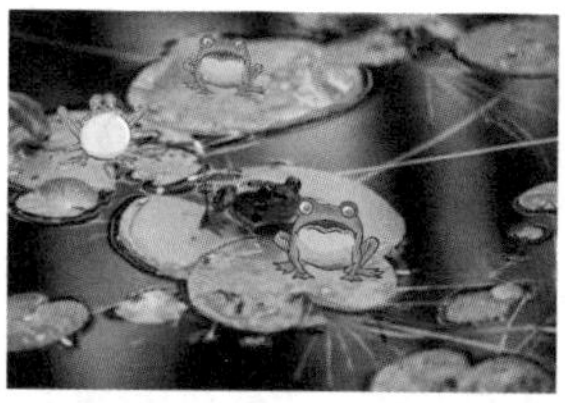

1) SENSORY LANGUAGE — This describes things you can touch, see, smell or hear. These make it all seem more real in your head (e.g. "festered" and "gargled").
2) CHILDISH LANGUAGE — This is used when the poet is talking about childhood. He uses long, rambling sentences, and words like "daddy" and "mammy".
3) MILITARY LANGUAGE — This is used when the poet sees the frogs enter the dam. They're now scary like war, not funny and innocent, like when he was young. (E.g. "grenades", "threats").

Remember the Feelings and Attitudes in the Poem

1) MEMORY — This poem is a memory of his feelings as a young boy.
2) EXCITEMENT — At first he's excited by the frogspawn (lines 8-10).
3) FEAR — Then the boy is frightened by the frogs taking over the flax-dam (lines 31-33).
4) SIGNIFICANCE — The poet, Seamus Heaney, looks back on this moment in his life as making a significant impact on his personality.

This poem is also about growing up. The poet sees the frogs differently from when he was in infants.

Think About Your Feelings and Attitudes to the Poem

1) Pick 2 words or phrases that stand out to you. If none stand out, just pick 2 unusual words or phrases.
2) Write these 2 words or phrases down. Then write about how they make you feel. If they don't make you feel anything, don't worry — just make something up, as long as it's not too stupid.

EXAMPLE The phrase on line 30 about the frogs, "their blunt heads farting", sounds disgusting and makes me feel sick. The phrase is very effective in helping the reader sympathise with the feelings of the character in the poem.

Themes — nature, getting older and first person...

Compare 'Death of a Naturalist' with other poems about the same themes: nature ('Blackberry-Picking' p.40-41 and 'Inversnaid' p.32-33), getting older ('Follower' p.50-51) and use of the first person ('On the Train' p.64-65, 'Cold Knap Lake' p.66-67 and 'The Man He Killed' p.16-17).

Key Poem

Digging

This suggests that his pen can be dangerous.

Digging

Between my finger and my thumb
The squat pen rests; snug as a gun.

This makes the pen sound ugly.

This is assonance — the 'u' is repeated. The short, sharp effect is like the noise of digging.

Under my window, a clean rasping sound
When the spade sinks into the gravelly ground:
My father, digging. I look down

Alliteration.

Till his straining rump among the flowerbeds
Bends low, comes up twenty years away
Stooping in rhythm through potato drills
Where he was digging.

As the poet watches his father digging, it brings back memories of him digging potatoes twenty years ago.

The coarse boot nestled on the lug, the shaft
Against the inside knee was levered firmly.
He rooted out tall tops, buried the bright edge deep
To scatter new potatoes that we picked
Loving their cool hardness in our hands.

This is tactile language. He's describing how they felt to touch.

The alliteration gives a digging rhythm.

By God, the old man could handle a spade.
Just like his old man.

This exclamation really stands out. It's as if the poet has said it out loud.

My grandfather cut more turf in a day
Than any other man on Toner's bog.
Once I carried him milk in a bottle
Corked sloppily with paper. He straightened up
To drink it, then fell to right away

This shows the family pride in digging — his grandfather was the best at it.

These memories also remind him of his grandfather digging. The skill is passed down through the generations.

His grandfather is so absorbed in digging that he ignores the poet.

Nicking and slicing neatly, heaving sods
Over his shoulder, going down and down
For the good turf. Digging.

These verbs mimic the sound of a spade digging.

The poet also goes down and down, through his memories, looking for good ideas.

The cold smell of potato mould, the squelch and slap
Of soggy peat, the curt cuts of an edge
Through living roots awaken in my head.
But I've no spade to follow men like them.

Onomatopoeia

Alliteration

The poet hasn't inherited this skill, and perhaps feels guilty about it.

This plays on two meanings of 'roots' — in the soil, and Heaney's family memories.

Between my finger and my thumb
The squat pen rests.
I'll dig with it.

This image is repeated from the first stanza, but now the poet sees his pen as a tool, not a weapon.

The poet draws a parallel between writing and digging. He uses his pen like a spade, to dig out memories and ideas.

POEM DICTIONARY
squat — short and wide

Digging

Key Poem

The poet is inside writing while his father digs the garden. The sight reminds him of seeing his father digging potatoes and his grandfather digging peat in the past. He isn't following in their footsteps, but he does "dig" out ideas with his pen.

You've Got To Know What Happens in the Poem

Lines 1-6 — The poet is sitting inside, writing, and watching his father digging outside.

Lines 7-24 — The poet describes his memories of his father and his grandfather.

Lines 25-27 — The poet describes his memories of what digging felt like.

Lines 28-31 — The poet goes back to describe what he does as a writer, and links this to the idea of digging.

Learn About the Three Types of Language

1) REFERENCES TO MEMORIES AND FEELINGS — The poet is watching his father digging in the flowerbed in the present. This brings back memories of his father digging potatoes, and his grandfather digging turf. The poet shows the pride he feels in their skill and hard work.
2) DESCRIPTIVE LANGUAGE — The poet uses alliteration to give the poem the rhythm of someone digging. The verbs he uses are very clean, sharp-sounding phrases, like "rooted out", "nicking and slicing".
3) THE POET'S THOUGHTS — Most of the poem is description, but there are a few lines where the poet writes down his thoughts more directly. These are particularly effective because of the way they break up the description, and because the poem ends with the realisation that his own skill is important too.

Remember the Feelings and Attitudes in the Poem

"I'm sure I buried it round here somewhere..."

1) RESPECT — The poet feels respect for his father and grandfather.
2) GUILT — He also feels guilty that he hasn't followed in their footsteps.
3) MEMORIES — He's got fond memories of his past.

Think about Heaney's attitude to his writing. In this poem he seems to wonder if digging is a more useful skill than writing.

Think About Your Feelings and Attitudes to the Poem

1) Pick 2 words or phrases that stand out to you. If none stand out, just pick 2 unusual words or phrases.
2) Write these 2 words or phrases down. Then write about how they make you feel. If they don't make you feel anything, don't worry — just make something up, as long as it's not too stupid.

EXAMPLE The phrases "cold smell of potato mould" and "squelch and slap / Of soggy peat" really bring to life the smells and sounds of digging in wet and muddy earth. It reminds me of the feeling of earth on my hands, which always makes me feel really cold, wet and dirty.

Themes — memory, parent/child relationships, characters...

Compare 'Digging' with other poems about the same themes: memory ('Cold Knap Lake' p.66-67 and 'Follower' p.50-51), parent/child relationships ('Mali' p.56-57 and 'The Affliction of Margaret' p.10-11) and strong characters ('Catrin' p.52-53 and 'The Village Schoolmaster' p.28-29).

Mid-Term Break

Mid-Term Break

I sat all morning in the college sick bay
Counting bells knelling classes to a close.
At two o'clock our neighbours drove me home.

In the porch I met my father crying–
He had always taken funerals in his stride–
And Big Jim Evans saying it was a hard blow.

The baby cooed and laughed and rocked the pram
When I came in, and I was embarrassed
By old men standing up to shake my hand

And tell me they were "sorry for my trouble".
Whispers informed strangers I was the eldest,
Away at school, as my mother held my hand

In hers and coughed out angry tearless sighs.
At ten o'clock the ambulance arrived
With the corpse, stanched and bandaged by the nurses.

Next morning I went up into the room. Snowdrops
And candles soothed the bedside; I saw him
For the first time in six weeks. Paler now,

Wearing a poppy bruise on his left temple,
He lay in the four foot box as in his cot.
No gaudy scars, the bumper knocked him clear.

A four foot box, a foot for every year.

The word 'knelling' is usually associated with bells at funerals.

The references to time add to the factual tone.

You can tell this is a very sad event because he says it's unusual to see him crying, even at a funeral.

This contrasts with his dead brother in lines 18-21.

This is just an expression people use, but read it again once you've finished the poem, and compare it with line 21.

He's embarrassed by the reactions of other people.

They're talking about the poet as if he wasn't there.

Compare his mother's emotions to those of his father in line 4.

Assonance

The time makes these events seem very matter-of-fact.

The candles and snowdrops are part of the grieving process. They're personified here.

Remember the title of the poem — the poet has been away at school until now.

This is very descriptive, in contrast to most of the poem. Poppies are normally associated with remembering the war dead.

This contrasts with the living baby in line 7.

"Gaudy" doesn't fit with the word "scars" so it really stands out — it's usually a cheerful word.

There's no emotion in this phrase, even though it describes a terrible accident.

The repetition of the numbers emphasises the tiny coffin, and we realise for the first time how young his brother was.

This is the only rhyme in the poem, which adds to the impact of the last line.

POEM DICTIONARY
knelling — the sound of bells ringing, usually for a funeral
stanched — made to stop bleeding

Mid-Term Break

This poem is about Heaney's memories of his brother's funeral. He comes home from boarding school and has to face the reactions of his family and neighbours, and see the corpse.

You've Got To Know What Happens in the Poem

Lines 1-3	He's at school waiting to be taken home.
Lines 4-13	He arrives home for the funeral and faces the reactions of his family and the other mourners.
Lines 14-15	His brother's body is brought home.
Lines 16-22	He goes to see his brother's body in the coffin.

Learn About the Three Types of Language

1) IMAGERY — The poem is very factual. So when the poet does use imagery, it really stands out, e.g. when he uses the phrase "poppy bruise" to describe his brother's wound.
2) DESCRIPTIONS OF PEOPLE'S REACTIONS — Heaney describes the reactions of "strangers" and of his family to the death. The detached descriptions help you to imagine the numbness he might have felt at the time, and how he was embarrassed by the attention.
3) REFERENCES TO TIME — There are several references to time, and time passing in this poem. This gives the impression of going through a ritual, but it also gives a sense of how time has stopped for the dead boy, especially in the last line, "a foot for every year" — he won't get any taller, or any older.

Remember the Feelings and Attitudes in the Poem

1) GRIEF — The poet is remembering his past grief.
2) ADOLESCENCE — As a boy he is embarrassed by the reactions of others.
3) SHOCK — There's a sense of being shocked and stunned when he views the corpse, and the feeling of everything stopping for the dead child.
4) RITUAL — He sees the importance of ritual in the grieving process, e.g. "snowdrops", and the fact that a terrible event still has a routine.

Think About Your Feelings and Attitudes to the Poem

1) Pick 2 words or phrases that stand out to you. If none stand out, just pick 2 unusual words or phrases.
2) Write these 2 words or phrases down. Then write about how they make you feel. If they don't make you feel anything, don't worry — just make something up, as long as it's not too stupid.

> **EXAMPLE** The phrases "the baby cooed and laughed and rocked the pram" and "He lay... as in his cot" make me feel really sad. The contrast between the baby, and Heaney's dead brother seems worse when you realise his brother was young enough to sleep in a cot.

Themes — death, getting older and strong emotions...

Compare 'Mid-Term Break' with other poems about the same themes: death ('October' p.62-63 and 'On my first Sonne' p.6-7), getting older ('Blackberry-Picking' p.40-41 and 'Death of a Naturalist' p.42-43) and strong emotions ('Catrin' p.52-53 and 'The Field Mouse' p.60-61)

Key Poem

Storm on the Island

This is a very strong, safe opening statement. Compare it to the last line of the poem.

The island seems barren — nothing grows there.

This is a metaphor — trees sound like they're wailing or singing in a storm.

This is an unusual combination of words, mixing the ideas of fear and safety.

This is language normally used to describe war.

Storm on the Island

We are prepared: we build our houses squat,
Sink walls in rock and roof them with good slate.
The wizened earth has never troubled us
With hay, so, as you can see, there are no stacks
Or stooks that can be lost. Nor are there trees
Which might prove company when it blows full
Blast: you know what I mean – leaves and branches
Can raise a tragic chorus in a gale
So that you can listen to the thing you fear
Forgetting that it pummels your house too.
But there are no trees, no natural shelter.
You might think that the sea is company,
Exploding comfortably down on the cliffs
But no: when it begins, the flung spray hits
The very windows, spits like a tame cat
Turned savage. We just sit tight while wind dives
And strafes invisibly. Space is a salvo.
We are bombarded by the empty air.
Strange, it is a huge nothing that we fear.

There's a lot of words about safety and security in the first two lines.

This is the first hint of fear in the poem — why are there no crops on the island?

The word "company" is used here and on line 12, to emphasise the loneliness.

The poem seems more scary because the poet is talking directly to <u>you</u>.

This is a very violent way to describe the wind.

This simile shows how familiar things become frightening during the storm.

All they can do is wait helplessly for the storm to end.

The storm is invisible, there's nothing solid there. This contrasts with the solid rock mentioned in the first two lines of the poem.

POEM DICTIONARY
wizened — dried up
stooks — a pile of sheaves (bundles) of corn
strafes — to rake with gunfire at close range, often from the air
salvo — lots of guns firing at once

Storm on the Island

Key Poem

This poem describes the effects of a fierce storm on the inhabitants of an island. They prepare for the storm, but once it starts, they feel scared anyway...

You've Got To Know What Happens in the Poem

Lines 1-5	The poet shows how the community thinks it is prepared for the storm.
Lines 6-13	This is where the poem starts to change from security to fear. It describes the power and the sounds of the storm itself.
Lines 14-19	This part describes the fear as the storm attacks the island.

Learn About the Three Types of Language

1) CONTRASTING DESCRIPTIONS OF SAFETY AND FEAR — The poem uses a lot of words to do with safety and security at the beginning of the poem. The tone changes though, and the sense of loneliness increases as familiar things become frightening during the storm.
2) DIRECT TONE — The poet involves you in his fear of the storm by speaking directly to "you", the reader.
3) IMAGERY — The poet creates word pictures of the storm using descriptive language, e.g. he uses the type of language normally used to describe war, to emphasise the violence of the storm.

Remember the Feelings and Attitudes in the Poem

1) SAFETY — The first part of the poem shows the community's feelings of safety, and preparation for the storm.
2) FEAR — This sense of security soon changes to fear, as familiar things change and become frightening.
3) HELPLESSNESS — The people can't do anything about their fear except wait for the storm to finish. This is a strong contrast to the start of the poem.

The first eight letters of the title spell STORMONT. Stormont Castle is an important location for Northern Irish politics. You could link the themes of fear and safety in this poem with the Northern Ireland conflict.

Think About Your Feelings and Attitudes to the Poem

1) Pick 2 words or phrases that stand out to you. If none stand out, just pick 2 unusual words or phrases.
2) Write these 2 words or phrases down. Then write about how they make you feel. If they don't make you feel anything, don't worry — just make something up, as long as it's not too stupid.

EXAMPLE The contrast between the phrase "We are prepared" and "it is a huge nothingness that we fear" makes me feel frightened. The solid assurance of the first few lines has been replaced at the end of the poem by fear of a frightening, invisible force.

Themes — nature, danger and imagery...

Compare 'Storm on the Island' with other poems about the same themes: nature ('Inversnaid' p.32-33 and 'Perch' p.38-39), danger ('The Little Boy Lost'/'The Little Boy Found' p.12-13 and 'Patrolling Barnegat p.18-19) and imagery ('October' p.62-63 and 'At a Potato Digging' p.36-37).

Follower

Follower

My father worked with a horse-plough,
His shoulders globed like a full sail strung
Between the shafts and the furrow.
The horses strained at his clicking tongue.

An expert. He would set the wing
And fit the bright steel-pointed sock.
The sod rolled over without breaking.
At the headrig, with a single pluck

Of reins, the sweating team turned round
And back into the land. His eye
Narrowed and angled at the ground,
Mapping the furrow exactly.

I stumbled in his hob-nailed wake,
Fell sometimes on the polished sod;
Sometimes he rode me on his back
Dipping and rising to his plod.

I wanted to grow up and plough,
To close one eye, stiffen my arm.
All I ever did was follow
In his broad shadow round the farm.

I was a nuisance, tripping, falling,
Yapping always. But today
It is my father who keeps stumbling
Behind me, and will not go away.

Simile.

This suggests tough, physical work

"Rolled" and "breaking" suggest waves of the sea.

This shows his father's level of skill and control.

This shows how skilled his father is.

This sounds a bit like someone navigating a ship

The poet found it hard to follow in his father's footsteps.

Uses language of the sea and sailing.

The regular rhythm of this line emphasises the child's movement on his father's back.

Each stanza has at least two lines which rhyme.

He felt like a failure, unable to keep up.

In line 13 the boy was stumbling behind his father. Now the roles are reversed.

This suggests that the poet would now quite like to leave his father behind — but he can't break the connection.

POEM DICTIONARY
globed — rounded (like a globe)
shafts — wooden poles which harness the animal to the plough
furrow — a long narrow trench made by the plough in the soil
wing — part of the frame of the plough
sock — the end of the plough that cuts the soil
sod — grass covered earth
headrig — the end of the ploughed part of the field where the horse has to turn round (also part of a ship's rigging)
sweating team — the horses pulling the plough

Follower

The poet remembers being a young boy following his father as he did the ploughing. Now he's older, he says the roles have reversed — his father follows him instead. He might mean that his father is now old and dependent. Or he might mean that his father is dead, and the memories won't go away.

You've Got To Know What Happens in the Poem

Lines 1-12 These lines describe the father's expert ploughing.

Lines 13-16 The narrator followed his father round the farm. Sometimes his father gave him a piggy-back.

Lines 17-22 These lines describe the narrator's sense of failure — he wanted to be like his father, but all he ever did was follow him around being a nuisance.

Lines 23-24 Now they're older, the relationship has been reversed, and now his father is the follower.

Learn About the Three Types of Language

1) SAILING IMAGERY — The poet uses images of sailing and the sea to show how his father looked when he was ploughing, e.g. "without breaking" likens the ploughed earth to waves on the sea.
2) LANGUAGE SHOWING SKILL AND CONTROL — The poet emphasises the skill his father had, controlling the straining horses with his "clicking tongue". This shows the admiration he felt for his father.
3) REFLECTIVE LANGUAGE — The poet sees himself through his father's eyes, as a "nuisance", and maybe a failure, but this is reversed in the last stanza, where his father is the one "stumbling / Behind".

Remember the Feelings and Attitudes in the Poem

Geoff dreamed of being a Roman chariot-racer.

1) ADMIRATION — The poet admires his father's skill at ploughing.
2) HERO-WORSHIP — As a child, he struggled to follow his father and hoped to take his place one day.
3) FEELINGS OF FAILURE — The poet worries that he is a failure because he didn't follow in his father's footsteps.
4) FAMILY TIES — The poet's relationship with his father is still important to him now that he's older — it "will not go away".

Think About Your Feelings and Attitudes to the Poem

1) Pick 2 words or phrases that stand out to you. If none stand out, just pick 2 unusual words or phrases.
2) Write these 2 words or phrases down. Then write about how they make you feel. If they don't make you feel anything, don't worry — just make something up, as long as it's not too stupid.

EXAMPLE The phrase "single pluck" shows how skilful the poet's father was at ploughing with horses. The phrase sounds like a sharp, sudden movement, which is emphasised by putting it at the end of the stanza. It makes me admire his father's skill, and understand why the poet wanted to be like him.

Themes — parent/child relationships, memory, characters...

Compare 'Follower' with other poems about the same themes: parent/child relationships ('Digging' p.44-45 and 'Catrin' p.52-53), memory ('Perch' p.38-39 and 'Cold Knap Lake' p.66-67) and strong characters ('Mid-Term Break' p.46-47 and 'The Song of the Old Mother' p.8-9).

Key Poem

Catrin

Gillian Clarke was born in 1937 in Cardiff. In 1990 she co-founded a writers' centre in North Wales called Ty Newydd. She teaches creative writing at the University of Glamorgan. Many of her poems reflect her cultural identity and family relationships in Wales.

Catrin

I can remember you, child,
As I stood in a hot, white
Room at the window watching
The people and cars taking
Turn at the traffic lights.
I can remember you, our first
Fierce confrontation, the tight
Red rope of love which we both
Fought over. It was a square
Environmental blank, disinfected
Of paintings or toys. I wrote
All over the walls with my
Words, coloured the clean squares
With the wild, tender circles
Of our struggle to become
Separate. We want, we shouted,
To be two, to be ourselves.

Neither won nor lost the struggle
In the glass tank clouded with feelings
Which changed us both. Still I am fighting
You off, as you stand there
With your straight, strong, long
Brown hair and your rosy,
Defiant glare, bringing up
From the heart's pool that old rope,
Tightening about my life,
Trailing love and conflict,
As you ask may you skate
In the dark, for one more hour.

The first line shows that the poet is talking personally and directly to her daughter.

The peace and normality of her life before the birth, contrasts with the conflict which follows.

Here she describes the umbilical cord as a bond of love between them.

She and her daughter were fighting each other even before she was born.

They are in competition with each other.

The shouts of pain fill the bare, simple room with emotion.

Suggests affection between parent and child.

Being on a separate line emphasises the importance of this word.

They are united in wanting to be separated.

Suggests the conflict between them still exists.

The glass tank (possibly an incubator) stands for their relationship — it's clouded up by their mixed feelings for each other.

She admires her daughter's strength and beauty.

Years later, they still haven't broken free from each other.

Suggests her daughter is always standing up to her.

The rope stands for her struggle with her daughter — and the mixed emotions of love and conflict this brings up.

This could be a metaphor for her uncertainty about her feelings towards her daughter.

The struggle seems set to continue.

POEM DICTIONARY
disinfected — cleaned

Catrin

Key Poem

In this poem, the poet talks to her daughter. She describes the struggle of the birth, and says that they're still struggling with each other years later. Like, guys, get over it ok...

You've Got To Know What Happens in the Poem

Lines 1-9 The poet tells her daughter about when she was born. She remembers staring out of the window (lines 1-5), before the difficulties of the birth (6-9).

Lines 9-17 The poet says the room she was in was clean, empty and soulless (9-11), until she "coloured" it with her shouts and screams during the birth. She says she and her daughter were both desperate to be separate from each other.

Lines 18-29 The poet says that they're still in a struggle with each other (18-20). She describes a more recent incident when her daughter, now a child, confronts her by asking if she can carry on skating. This makes the poet feel a similar sense of conflict to when her daughter was born.

Learn About the Three Types of Language

1) CONFRONTATIONAL LANGUAGE — Both mother and daughter are desperate to break free from each other. The birth is described as a violent struggle to break apart, and they're still in conflict years later.
2) LOVING LANGUAGE — There are signs of the poet's love for her daughter. These feelings of affection often seem to be a result of being physically close — they have an intense, natural bond.
3) METAPHORICAL LANGUAGE — Rope seems to mean the umbilical cord — but it's also used as a symbol of love and of the power struggle between mother and daughter.

Remember the Feelings and Attitudes in the Poem

AAAAAAAARRRRRRGGGHHHH!!!

1) CONFLICT — The poet feels aggression between her and her daughter.
2) LOVE — She also feels affection and motherly love.
3) CONFUSION — She shows that these mixed feelings have always been there — and maybe they always will.

The poet's feelings for her daughter are confused. She's torn between hostility and love.

Think About Your Feelings and Attitudes to the Poem

1) Pick 2 words or phrases that stand out to you. If none stand out, just pick 2 unusual words or phrases.
2) Write these 2 words or phrases down. Then write about how they make you feel. If they don't make you feel anything, don't worry — just make something up, as long as it's not too stupid.

EXAMPLE The phrase "the tight / Red rope of love" makes me feel sympathy for the narrator. She seems very confused by her feelings, as the love she feels for her daughter seems to strangle and hurt her. It is hard to see how they will resolve their conflict.

Themes — parent/child relationship, love, strong emotions...

Compare 'Catrin' with other poems about the same themes: parent/child relationships ('Digging' p.44-45 and 'Follower' p.50-51), love ('On my first Sonne' p.6-7 and 'Sonnet 130' p.20-21) and strong emotions ('Mid-Term Break' p.46-47 and 'The Affliction of Margaret' p.10-11).

Baby-sitting

Baby-sitting

I am sitting in a strange room listening
For the wrong baby. I don't love
This baby. She is sleeping a snuffly
Roseate, bubbling sleep; she is fair;
She is a perfectly acceptable child.
I am afraid of her. If she wakes
She will hate me. She will shout
Her hot midnight rage, her nose
Will stream disgustingly and the perfume
Of her breath will fail to enchant me.

To her I will represent absolute
Abandonment. For her it will be worse
Than for the lover cold in lonely
Sheets; worse than for the woman who waits
A moment to collect her dignity
Beside the bleached bone in the terminal ward.
As she rises sobbing from the monstrous land
Stretching for milk-familiar comforting,
She will find me and between us two
It will not come. It will not come.

There's an unnatural feel to the whole situation for her.

The factual, straightforward tone seems shockingly uncaring.

Short sentences — she sounds calm and certain.

The stress falls on this word due to being on a new line.

Another image of betrayed love.

The baby's need for her mother's milk seems natural and right.

She sees herself as a poor substitute for the baby's mother, with nothing to offer.

The baby is snug and happy while she's asleep.

Unemotional, uncaring way of describing a baby.

She can only think of the worst things about babies.

Sarcastically describes the baby's smell.

Says an abandoned baby feels even worse than someone who's suffered a bereavement.

She thinks the baby has been having nightmares.

Repetition shows her absolute certainty that she can't comfort the baby.

POEM DICTIONARY
roseate — happy, rose-coloured

Baby-sitting

The poet writes about her feelings when baby-sitting someone else's child. She doesn't love the baby she's looking after because it's not hers. She's worried that when the baby wakes up, she won't be able to give her the comfort she needs, because her mother isn't there. So sad...

You've Got To Know What Happens in the Poem

Lines 1-5 — The poet says she's looking after someone else's baby in a house which isn't hers. The baby is sleeping.

Lines 6-10 — She's scared that when the baby wakes up, she'll be all noisy, snotty and disgusting.

Lines 11-16 — The poet says that when the baby sees her, she'll feel horribly abandoned because her mum isn't there.

Lines 17-20 — She says that the baby will want her mother's milk — but she won't get it.

Learn About the Three Types of Language

1) DRY TONE — At times she sounds emotionless. She feels detached (separated) from the baby, and seems to see it as an object and a problem, rather than a person.
2) BLEAK LANGUAGE — The poet has a very pessimistic outlook — she predicts nothing but the worst, e.g. that the baby will feel abandoned when she wakes up. The poet sees no way of avoiding this.
3) IMAGERY — There are some pretty depressing images — the poet uses them to describe how awful she thinks the baby will feel when it wakes up and finds its mum isn't there.

Remember the Feelings and Attitudes in the Poem

"Are you old enough to be looking after me?"

1) DISCOMFORT — She feels really uncomfortable, in the "strange room" with the "wrong baby".
2) FEAR — She's scared that she won't be able to give the baby what it needs.
3) SORROW — She feels despair at the "Abandonment" of the baby.

She completely focuses on the negatives of baby-sitting — ignoring the more positive aspects, like getting paid for basically watching TV and texting your mates.

Think About Your Feelings and Attitudes to the Poem

1) Pick 2 words or phrases that stand out to you. If none stand out, just pick 2 unusual words or phrases.
2) Write these 2 words or phrases down. Then write about how they make you feel. If they don't make you feel anything, don't worry — just make something up, as long as it's not too stupid.

EXAMPLE I find the phrase "I don't love / This baby" shocking. The baby-sitter does not seem to feel any emotions at all for the baby, but I would expect anyone looking after a baby to feel at least something for it.

Themes — imagery, first person and strong emotions...

Compare 'Baby-sitting' with other poems about similar themes: imagery ('At a Potato Digging' p.36-37 and 'On the Train' p.64-65), use of the first person ('Follower' p.50-51 and 'On my first Sonne' p.6-7) and strong emotions ('Mid-Term Break' p.46-47 and 'Catrin' p.52-53).

Mali

Mali

Three years ago to the hour, the day she was born,
that unmistakable brim and tug of the tide
I'd thought was over. I drove
the twenty miles of summer lanes,
my daughter cursing Sunday cars,
and the lazy swish of a dairy herd
rocking so slowly home.

Something in the event,
late summer heat overspilling into harvest,
apples reddening on heavy trees,
the lanes sweet with brambles
and our fingers purple,
then the child coming easy,
too soon, in the wrong place,

things seasonal and out of season
towed home a harvest moon.
My daughter's daughter
a day old under an umbrella on the beach
late-comer at summer's festival,
and I'm hooked again, life-sentenced.
Even the sea could not draw me from her.

This year I bake her a cake like our house,
and old trees blossom
with balloons and streamers.
We celebrate her with a cup
of cold blue ocean,
candles at twilight, and three drops of,
probably, last blood.

The poet feels like she did when her daughter was born. She didn't think she'd have this kind of feeling again.

Natural forces indicate the birth is about to happen.

Suggests that you can't control the pace of nature.

The apples are about to fall off, as the baby is ready to be born.

The birth is compared to ripe fruit being picked at harvest time.

Vivid natural colours.

Read these 2 lines together — the lines in the middle describe the scene.

She's born early, before they can get to hospital.

The premature birth is like a plant growing in the wrong season.

She has no choice in loving her granddaughter, just like when her own daughter was born.

Sounds like nature is throwing a party.

Their natural bond is stronger than the tides mentioned in line 2.

This could mean the poet finding new joy in her life.

Colourful decorations to celebrate Mali's birthday.

Celebrate everything about Mali, not just the fact that it's her birthday.

One for each year of her life.

Blood represents the family line. The poet thinks this will be the last time she sees a new addition to her family.

POEM DICTIONARY
harvest moon — a full moon in autumn
twilight — fading light after sunset

Mali

This poem is about the birth of the poet's granddaughter, called Mali. The poet compares the birth to the summer harvest, and describes how she felt an intense love for Mali like she did when her own daughter was born.

You've Got To Know What Happens in the Poem

Lines 1-7 On her granddaughter Mali's third birthday, the poet remembers driving her daughter to hospital to give birth to Mali. But they get held up on a country lane.

Lines 8-14 The poet remembers the scene. It's summer, with the harvest beginning and lots of colour all around. The baby was born quickly, before they arrived at hospital.

Lines 15-21 When Mali was just a day old, the poet felt an incredibly strong bond with her.

Lines 22-28 The family celebrate at Mali's third birthday party. The poet says Mali will probably be the last new addition to the family in the poet's lifetime.

Learn About the Three Types of Language

1) NATURAL LANGUAGE — The birth is linked to the moon, tides and the images of the countryside that surround it. The ripe fruit of the harvest is compared to the baby.
2) NEW LIFE — The events are familiar to the poet — they remind her of when she gave birth to her daughter. The birth of her granddaughter is the start of a new phase in the life cycle of the family.
3) LANGUAGE OF CELEBRATION — There's joy at the birth of the child, and it seems as if nature is part of the celebration. At the end of the poem they celebrate her third birthday.

Remember the Feelings and Attitudes in the Poem

1) JOY — She's happy at the birth of her granddaughter, and she loves her.
2) APPREHENSION — But she's also apprehensive about her — she thinks there'll be bad times as well as good (line 20).
3) CONNECTION — She feels a strong connection with nature, because of the birth and her memories of giving birth herself.

Think About Your Feelings and Attitudes to the Poem

1) Pick 2 words or phrases that stand out to you. If none stand out, just pick 2 unusual words or phrases.
2) Write these 2 words or phrases down. Then write about how they make you feel. If they don't make you feel anything, don't worry — just make something up, as long as it's not too stupid.

> **EXAMPLE** When the poet says "Even the sea could not draw me from her", I really admire her. It seems that she will always be there for her granddaughter, which I think is really brave, as she knows it will not be easy.

Themes — nature, memory and imagery...

Compare 'Mali' with other poems about the same themes: nature ('Blackberry-Picking' p.40-41 and 'Sonnet' p.34-35), memory ('Perch' p.38-39 and 'Digging' p.44-45) and imagery ('Death of a Naturalist' p.42-43 and 'The Field-Mouse' p.60-61).

Key Poem

A Difficult Birth, Easter 1998

A Difficult Birth, Easter 1998

An old ewe that somehow till this year
had given the ram the slip. We thought her barren.
Good Friday, and the Irish peace deal close,
and tonight she's serious, restless and hoofing the straw.
We put off the quiet supper and bottle of wine
we'd planned, to celebrate if the news is good.

Her waters broke an hour ago and she's sipped
her own lost salty ocean from the ground.
While they slog it out in Belfast, eight decades
since Easter 1916, exhausted, tamed by pain,
she licks my fingers with a burning tongue,
lies down again. Two hooves and a muzzle.

But the lamb won't come. You phone for help
and step into the lane to watch for car lights.
This is when the whitecoats come to the women,
well-meaning, knowing best, with their needles and forceps.
So I ease my fingers in, take the slippery head
in my right hand, two hooves in my left.

We strain together, harder than we dared.
I feel a creak in the limbs and pull till he comes
in a syrupy flood. She drinks him, famished, and you find us
peaceful, at a cradling that might have been a death.
Then the second lamb slips through her opened door,
the stone rolled away.

The Good Friday Agreement was a famous peace agreement in Northern Ireland. In Christianity, Good Friday is the date of Christ's death, before his resurrection.

They'd given up hope of the ewe having lambs — just as some had given up hope of peace in Northern Ireland.

Like the Last Supper — Jesus' last meal with his disciples.

A sign that she's ready to give birth.

This refers to both the situation in Belfast, and the ewe.

This is when the troubles in Northern Ireland first broke out.

The lamb is stuck, like the peace talks in Northern Ireland.

Looking for a sign of hope.

This could stand for the need for people to get personally involved in resolving difficult situations, instead of relying on other people.

Doctors helping women experiencing difficult births.

The poet and the ewe struggle together for a common goal — like the different sides in the Irish peace process, pulling together for the first time.

The lamb is small and vulnerable — it's a fragile peace.

Christians believe that when the stone at the entrance to Christ's tomb was rolled away, it was a sign of his resurrection.

Jesus is sometimes called "The Lamb of God".

Both the physical chance for the second lamb to be born, and the chance for peace.

POEM DICTIONARY

ewe — female sheep
ram — male sheep
barren — unable to have children
Good Friday — in Christianity, this is the day of Christ's death, before his resurrection on Easter Sunday.
Belfast — capital of Northern Ireland, where there have been violent troubles between Catholics and Protestants since 1916
forceps — tool used to help deliver babies

A Difficult Birth, Easter 1998

Key Poem

This poem describes an old sheep giving birth. It's a struggle against the odds, but in the end the lambs are born safely. This is used as a metaphor for the struggle for peace in Northern Ireland.

You've Got To Know What Happens in the Poem

Lines 1-6	An old sheep is in pain — she's about to give birth to her first lambs.
Lines 7-12	The poet describes the peace talks in Belfast, and the ewe's difficulties in giving birth.
Lines 13-18	They call for help, but none arrives. The poet thinks of when people try to help women give birth. She reaches in to try to pull the lamb out.
Lines 19-24	After a struggle, the lamb is born safely. Then another one arrives — bonus.

Learn About the Three Types of Language

1) WAR and PEACE — The birth of the lambs stands for the birth of peace in Northern Ireland. The poet refers to the peace talks in Belfast, which are going on at the time of the birth.
2) RELIGIOUS REFERENCES — Easter is significant for Christians — it's the time when Christ died and was resurrected (born again). In the poem, this religious symbol of new life is linked to the unexpected birth of the lambs and also peace after all the troubles. It's also relevant because the troubles in Northern Ireland were based partly around religion (conflict between Catholics and Protestants).
3) METAPHORICAL LANGUAGE — The details of the birth are a metaphor for the difficulties and eventual breakthrough in the Good Friday Agreement in Belfast.

Remember the Feelings and Attitudes in the Poem

Sheep — bringers of wool and peace.

1) WORRY — She's worried about the sheep and lamb, and about the situation in Northern Ireland.
2) RELIEF — She's relieved and happy when the birth and the peace talks turn out all right.

The religious references could suggest she sees the birth and the peace agreement as miracles — they seemed impossible, like the resurrection of Christ.

Think About Your Feelings and Attitudes to the Poem

1) Pick 2 words or phrases that stand out to you. If none stand out, just pick 2 unusual words or phrases.
2) Write these 2 words or phrases down. Then write about how they make you feel. If they don't make you feel anything, don't worry — just make something up, as long as it's not too stupid.

EXAMPLE When I first read the line, "We strain together, harder than we dared", I felt very nervous. The poet and the ewe are pulling together to try to bring about a happy outcome. It brings home to me just how tense the peace talks must have been.

Themes — politics, nature and imagery...

Compare 'A Difficult Birth, Easter 1998' with other poems about the same themes: politics ('At a Potato Digging' p.36-37 and 'The Field-Mouse' p.60-61), nature ('Storm on the Island' p.48-49 and 'Perch' p.38-39) and imagery ('Digging' p.44-45 and 'Tichborne's Elegy' p.14-15).

Key Poem

The Field-Mouse

The Field-Mouse

Summer, and the long grass is a snare drum.
The air hums with jets.
Down at the end of the meadow,
far from the radio's terrible news,
we cut the hay. All afternoon
its wave breaks before the tractor blade.
Over the hedge our neighbour travels his field
in a cloud of lime, drifting our land
with a chance gift of sweetness.

The child comes running through the killed flowers,
his hands a nest of quivering mouse,
its black eyes two sparks burning.
We know it will die and ought to finish it off.
It curls in agony big as itself
and the star goes out in its eye.
Summer in Europe, the field's hurt,
and the children kneel in long grass,
staring at what we have crushed.

Before day's done the field lies bleeding,
the dusk garden inhabited by the saved, voles,
frogs, a nest of mice. The wrong that woke
from a rumour of pain won't heal,
and we can't face the newspapers.
All night I dream the children dance in grass
their bones brittle as mouse-ribs, the air
stammering with gunfire, my neighbour turned
stranger, wounding my land with stones.

The scene appears peaceful at the start of the poem.

Makes the harvest sound violent — linking it to the bombs.

Their neighbour is peaceful and pleasant.

The child wants to protect the mouse.

Pain takes over its whole body.

The chopping of the hay is perhaps compared to the bombs in former-Yugoslavia.

These animals are the equivalent to the survivors of the bombings.

Her children are as weak and vulnerable as the mouse in the field.

Onomatopoeia is used to describe the guns.

Metaphor

Double meaning — "snare" also means "trap".

Here the jets are harmless, but in Europe they bring bombs and destruction.

They feel completely separate from the war at this stage.

Sign of the harvest's destruction.

The last signs of life fade away.

Use of "we" suggests the war is our joint responsibility.

The field is personified — the harvest has killed it.

They can't face finding out about the full horror of the war.

In her dream, her neighbour has turned into her enemy — just as neighbours in former-Yugoslavia have done.

POEM DICTIONARY
lime — a substance used to make fields better for growing crops

The Field-Mouse

Key Poem

This poem is set at harvest time on a farm. It's the early 90s, and war is going on abroad in the former-Yugoslavia. The poet's family are cutting hay on the farm, when a mouse which has been hurt in the harvest makes the poet think of the innocent victims of the war abroad.

You've Got To Know What Happens in the Poem

Lines 1-6	The poet and other people are cutting the hay in their field.
Lines 7-9	The owner of the field next door adds lime to his field, sending a sweet smell over the hedge.
Lines 10-18	A child runs over with a dying mouse, which has been hurt in the hay-cutting. This is compared to children being killed by bombs in former-Yugoslavia.
Lines 19-23	At the end of the day, they've finished cutting the hay. They've heard about what's happened in former-Yugoslavia, but can't face reading about the details.
Lines 24-27	The poet has a nightmare about her neighbour attacking her land and children.

Learn About the Three Types of Language

1) IDEALISTIC LANGUAGE — The harvesters' life seems peaceful. At first they feel like they're separate from events elsewhere — until the poet starts making connections between the harvest and the war.
2) VIOLENT LANGUAGE — The chopping down of the hay comes to stand for the war in former-Yugoslavia. The brutality and cruelty of the war is shocking.
3) METAPHORICAL LANGUAGE — The mouse's death from the harvest is a metaphor for the innocent children dying in the war.

Remember the Feelings and Attitudes in the Poem

1) CONCERN — The poet is worried about the children in former-Yugoslavia.
2) GUILT — She feels guilty and responsible for what's happening (line 18).
3) FEAR — She's scared of just how bad the situation there might be (line 23).

In her nightmare, she's scared that her own children will suffer in the same way as the children in former-Yugoslavia.

Think About Your Feelings and Attitudes to the Poem

1) Pick 2 words or phrases that stand out to you. If none stand out, just pick 2 unusual words or phrases.
2) Write these 2 words or phrases down. Then write about how they make you feel. If they don't make you feel anything, don't worry — just make something up, as long as it's not too stupid.

EXAMPLE The description of the poet's children as having "bones brittle as mouse-ribs" makes me realise how helpless the victims of war are. I find this really scary and shocking as, even though this is a dream, the poet shows that this situation could happen anywhere.

Themes — politics, danger and imagery...

Compare 'The Field-Mouse' with other poems about the same themes: politics ('At a Potato Digging' p.36-37 and 'A Difficult Birth, Easter 1998' p.58-59), danger ('Storm on the Island' p.48-49 and 'Patrolling Barnegat' p.18-19) and imagery ('Blackberry-Picking' p.40-41 and 'Sonnet' p.34-35).

October

We know from the title that the poem is set in autumn.

The broken branch is personified like it's part of a dead person.

The trees sound old and frail as they take on their autumn colours.

Bluntly tells us what's happening.

The weather is linked to the sadness of the people at the funeral.

Double meaning — the pen moves over the page, but it could also mean "later on".

This could mean that for a moment she doesn't want to be alive.

Simile.

October

Wind in the poplars and a broken branch,
a dead arm in the bright trees. Five poplars
tremble gradually to gold. The stone face
of the lion darkens in a sharp shower,
his dreadlocks of lobelia grown long,
tangled, more brown now than blue-eyed.

My friend dead and the graveyard at Orcop –
her short ride to the hawthorn hedge, lighter
than hare-bones on men's shoulders, our faces
stony, rain, weeping in the air. The grave
deep as a well takes the earth's thud, the slow
fall of flowers.

Over the page the pen
runs faster than wind's white steps over grass.
For a while health feels like pain. Then panic
running the fields, the grass, the racing leaves
ahead of light, holding that robin's eye
in the laurel, hydrangeas' faded green.
I must write like the wind, year after year
passing my death-day, winning ground.

The theme of death is introduced.

Alliteration emphasises the sound of the rain.

The overgrown plants look like tangled hair.

Going back to nature.

The sound of the earth hitting the coffin is shocking.

This could suggest she's running away from death.

There's an urgent, hurried feel to this stanza.

More reminders of autumn.

She wants to achieve as much as she can before she dies.

POEM DICTIONARY
poplars — a type of tall tree
lobelia — a type of plant with coloured flowers
laurel — the name of a type of small evergreen tree
hydrangeas — a type of tree with coloured flowers

October

This poem is about the funeral of one of the poet's friends. There are lots of images of autumn, which make the poet think about death — she's in the autumn years of her life. The poet thinks she may not be alive for all that much longer, so has to make the most of what life she has left.

You've Got To Know What Happens in the Poem

Lines 1-6 The poet describes an autumnal scene, with bare, broken trees and an overgrown sculpture.

Lines 7-12 She's at the funeral of a friend. It rains as her friend is buried.

Lines 12-19 The poet realises that she'll die too, and has to write as much as she can before she dies.

Learn About the Three Types of Language

1) LANGUAGE ABOUT DEATH — As well as the fact that there's a funeral going on, the theme of death is suggested by the dead branch of a tree and faded colours.
2) AUTUMNAL LANGUAGE — The bad weather and autumnal colours emphasise the idea of death at the funeral. Images of autumn also remind the poet that she is in the autumn years of her life.
3) NATURE — The poet describes nature in detail — using it to represent both death and her need to go on living (line 18).

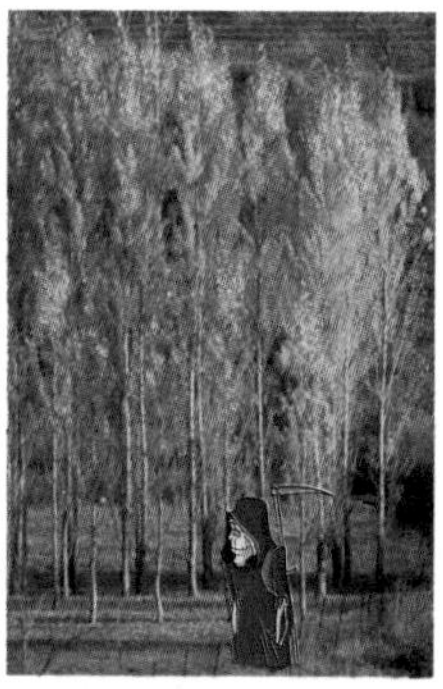

Remember the Feelings and Attitudes in the Poem

1) SADNESS — The poet is sad about the death of her friend.
2) FEAR — She's worried that she doesn't have long left to live herself.
3) DETERMINATION — She's determined to do as much as possible with the time she has left.

Think About Your Feelings and Attitudes to the Poem

1) Pick 2 words or phrases that stand out to you. If none stand out, just pick 2 unusual words or phrases.
2) Write these 2 words or phrases down. Then write about how they make you feel. If they don't make you feel anything, don't worry — just make something up, as long as it's not too stupid.

EXAMPLE The description of "rain, weeping in the air" makes me feel sad. It feels like the whole world, even the weather, is mourning for the loss of the poet's friend. It also makes it seem that death is always around us, wherever we are.

Themes — death, nature and imagery...

Compare 'October' with other poems about the same themes: death ('Mid-Term Break' p.46-47 and 'On my first Sonne' p.6-7), nature ('Perch' p.38-39 and 'Inversnaid' p.32-33), and imagery ('At a Potato Digging' p.36-37 and 'Mali' p.56-57).

On the Train

The train the poet is on protects its passengers like they're children.

Double meaning — a "black box" is sometimes used to find out what's caused a crash.

The radio is personified as the bringer of bad news.

No one knows the details yet — they're in the dark.

Could mean that people on other trains are unaware of what's happened.

A recorded message as they can't get through to loved ones — a bad sign.

Animal-like cry of distress when there's no response.

Usually an empty statement, but now has an important meaning — she's safe.

On the Train

Cradled through England between flooded fields
rocking, rocking the rails, my head-phones on,
the black box of my Walkman on the table.
Hot tea trembles in its plastic cup.
I'm thinking of you waking in our bed
thinking of me on the train. Too soon to phone.

The radio speaks in the suburbs, in commuter towns,
in cars unloading children at school gates,
is silenced in dark parkways down the line
before locks click and footprints track the frost
and trains slide out of stations in the dawn
dreaming their way towards the blazing bone-ship.

The Vodafone you are calling
may have been switched off.
Please call later. And calling later,
calling later their phones ring in the rubble
and in the rubble of suburban kitchens
the wolves howl into silent telephones.

I phone. No answer. Where are you now?
The train moves homeward through the morning.
Tonight I'll be home safe, but talk to me, please.
Pick up the phone. Today I'm tolerant
of mobiles. Let them say it. I'll say it too.
Darling, I'm on the train.

Alliteration and rhythm create an impression of the sound of the train.

Suggests the fear that others will be feeling.

She wants to phone, but feels she should wait.

News of the crash spreads quickly.

Awful image — like a shipwreck. Contrasts with the sleepy quietness of the lines that come before.

Meaning changes from the rubble of the crash to the rubble of people's lives, wrecked by what's happened.

Short sentences make her sound anxious.

She's desperate to get in touch.

POEM DICTIONARY
commuter towns — towns where people live but travel to work somewhere else every day

On the Train

The poet is travelling by train on the day of the Paddington train crash in 1999. She tries to phone her husband so that he doesn't worry about her, but she can't get through to him. She thinks of all the people who'll be anxiously phoning up loved ones to find out if they're ok.

You've Got To Know What Happens in the Poem

Lines 1-6 The poet is travelling on a train. She thinks of her husband waking up, wondering if she's ok.

Lines 7-12 She describes the news of the crash reaching people across the country.

Lines 13-18 Friends and relatives of people who might be on the train which has crashed try to phone them — but can't get through.

Lines 19-24 The poet tries to phone her husband to say she's ok, but she can't get through either.

Learn About the Three Types of Language

1) FEARFUL LANGUAGE — The poet imagines the fear people must be going through as they try to phone their loved ones. When phones aren't answered, it seems to be a terrible sign.
2) REFERENCES TO TECHNOLOGY — Mobile phones are an important theme — the poet imagines people using them to try and find out their loved ones are ok. For once mobiles have a serious use — phrases which are usually just annoying, like "I'm on the train", become important and meaningful.
3) METAPHORICAL LANGUAGE — Trains are described as if they're protective and comforting at the start of the poem, but deadly later on. The desperate cries of relatives are described as the howls of wolves.

Remember the Feelings and Attitudes in the Poem

1) ANXIETY — The poet is worried that her husband will think she's been hurt in the crash.
2) DESPERATION — She's desperate to get in touch with him.
3) EMPATHY — She feels sorry for all the people who are worrying about loved ones.

The poet is anxious to let her husband know she's all right, but thinks of those who won't receive such good news.

Think About Your Feelings and Attitudes to the Poem

1) Pick 2 words or phrases that stand out to you. If none stand out, just pick 2 unusual words or phrases.
2) Write these 2 words or phrases down. Then write about how they make you feel. If they don't make you feel anything, don't worry — just make something up, as long as it's not too stupid.

EXAMPLE I find the line "the wolves howl into silent telephones" shocking and horrifying. It creates a terrible image of how devastated the relatives of the victims of the crash are feeling. They are unable to do anything but scream in terror, like wild animals.

Themes — death, first person, language effects...

Compare 'On the Train' with other poems about the same themes: death ('Mid-Term Break' p.46-47 and 'October' p.62-63), use of the first person ('Baby-sitting' p.54-55 and 'The Man He Killed' p.16-17) and language effects ('Perch' p.38-39 and 'At a Potato Digging' p.36-37).

Key Poem — Cold Knap Lake

Cold Knap Lake

We once watched a crowd
pull a drowned child from the lake.
Blue-lipped and dressed in water's long green silk
she lay for dead.

Then kneeling on the earth,
a heroine, her red head bowed,
her wartime cotton frock soaked,
my mother gave a stranger's child her breath.
The crowd stood silent,
drawn by the dread of it.

The child breathed, bleating
and rosy in my mother's hands.
My father took her home to a poor house
and watched her thrashed for almost drowning.

Was I there?
Or is that troubled surface something else
shadowy under the dipped fingers of willows
where satiny mud blooms in cloudiness
after the treading, heavy webs of swans
as their wings beat and whistle on the air?

All lost things lie under closing water
in that lake with the poor man's daughter.

Sounds like she's dead at this point.

She's covered in pond weeds. The "silk" contrasts with her "poor house" (line 13).

Dramatic descriptions of her mother's bravery.

Her mother's actions while giving mouth-to-mouth make it sound like she's praying.

A selfless act — she clearly admires her mother for it.

Alliteration adds to the drama of the story.

Transformation, from death to life — as if the poet's mother has performed a miracle.

A shocking image, but the poet sounds unemotional.

Short line makes it sound like she's stopped to think about it.

The surface of the lake — but also her uncertain memory.

What she saw was dark and vague — her imagination might have created the story from her uncertain memory.

The water was muddy and unclear, like the memory.

These lines bring together the points she's been discussing, and answer the questions she's been asking herself.

Rhyming couplet brings the poem to a neat conclusion.

POEM DICTIONARY
satiny — smooth, glossy (like satin)

Cold Knap Lake

Key Poem

The poet describes a time when her mother rescued a drowning girl from a lake. Then she wonders whether the memory is real or not. Place your bets...

You've Got To Know What Happens in the Poem

Lines 1-4 The poet remembers seeing a crowd gathered around a girl who's just been pulled out of a lake.

Lines 5-12 She describes how her mother saved the girl by giving her mouth-to-mouth resuscitation.

Lines 13-14 The poet's father took the girl home, where she was beaten by her own father.

Lines 15-22 The poet wonders whether the memory is real — it could have been something else in the muddy lake. She says memories often become confused.

Learn About the Two Types of Language

1) DRAMATIC LANGUAGE — The poet's descriptions of how her mother revived the girl make the story sound almost too amazing to be true. This is maybe why the poet wonders if she's imagined it.
2) PHILOSOPHICAL LANGUAGE — The poet questions herself and wonders about how memories work. The uncertain language in the last two verses adds to the idea that things might not have actually happened as she remembers them. She tries to come up with some answers to tie things together.

Remember the Feelings and Attitudes in the Poem

Real or imaginary?

1) ADMIRATION — The poet admires her mother for saving the girl.
2) CONFUSION — She's confused about what's real and what's imagined.
3) WONDER — She's fairly philosophical at the end of the poem — she says that memories can get blurred, and that's just how it is.

The feel of the poem changes sharply at line 15 — it starts off with dramatic, vivid images, then changes to an uncertain, wondering tone.

Think About Your Feelings and Attitudes to the Poem

1) Pick 2 words or phrases that stand out to you. If none stand out, just pick 2 unusual words or phrases.
2) Write these 2 words or phrases down. Then write about how they make you feel. If they don't make you feel anything, don't worry — just make something up, as long as it's not too stupid.

EXAMPLE I find the phrase "satiny mud blooms in cloudiness" really interesting. It is a very clever way of describing how memories can become muddled and unclear.

Themes — memory, danger, closing couplet...

Compare 'Cold Knap Lake' with other poems about the same themes: memory ('Digging' p.44-45 and 'Catrin' p.52-53), danger ('Storm on the Island' p.48-49 and 'The Field-Mouse' p.60-61) and use of a closing couplet ('Sonnet 130' p.20-21 and 'The Village Schoolmaster' p.28-29).

Nature

Loads of poets write about nature. Sometimes it's just because they like the countryside. Other times it's because they see nature as a metaphor for all the other stuff going on in their life.

1) The beauty and power of nature can be exciting.
2) Nature can also be cruel and destructive — a threat to human life.
3) Nature needs to be treated with respect and not taken for granted.

Some Poets Celebrate Nature's Beauty

Inversnaid (Pages 32-33)

1) The poet loves the scene he describes. He feels protective of it — "Long live the weeds and the wilderness yet".
2) He finds beauty in a scene which is pretty bleak and wild — the muddy river is described as a "darksome burn, horseback brown", and the foam on the water as a "windpuff-bonnet".

Sonnet (Pages 34-35)

1) The poet describes the countryside in summer.
2) He describes the colours of nature — the "white wool sack clouds" and the "Mare blobs stain with gold the meadow drain". This helps the reader imagine the beauty of the scene.
3) He describes the wildlife in the scene with a lot of affection: "the Moor Hen", the "bright beetles" and the "insects happy wings". This shows that he's observed the scene in detail: he really cares about it.

Some Poets write about the Power of Nature

Mali (Pages 56-57)

1) In this poem, Clarke links the birth of her granddaughter with nature.
2) Her granddaughter's birth reminds her of her daughter's birth — it's a cycle of new life.
3) She describes the birth as like the "unmistakable brim and tug of the tide". It's part of an old, familiar pattern, as inevitable as the tide going in and out.
4) Her love for her new granddaughter is compared to the strength of nature: "Even the sea could not draw me from her".

Storm on the Island (Pages 48-49)

1) The poet uses the language of war to stress the sheer strength of the storm, e.g. "Exploding", "strafes" and "bombarded".
2) He shows how the people who live on the island are vulnerable and at the mercy of the storm. There is "no natural shelter".
3) The poet says you shouldn't underestimate the power of nature. It can be "like a tame cat / Turned savage" — turning on you when you least expect it.

She may look cute, but she'll get you.

The Eagle (Pages 24-25)

1) The poet creates a striking picture of a creature of tremendous power — "like a thunderbolt he falls".
2) He shows the eagle is dominant over his surroundings — "The wrinkled sea beneath him crawls".

Look out the window...

Clarke and Heaney both describe nature in several of their poems, often using it as a metaphor. Other poems about nature are: 'Patrolling Barnegat' (p.18-19), 'At a Potato Digging' (p.36-37), 'Perch' (p.38-39), 'Digging' (p.44-45), 'The Field-Mouse' (p.60-61) and 'October' (p.62-63).

Death

Death is something people feel emotional about — so it's a good theme for poetry.

1) The death of a loved one causes grief and a sense of loss.
2) Everyone dies — it's something we need to prepare for.
3) Deaths caused by war, crime or execution can seem an unnecessary waste of life.
4) Sometimes people kill out of anger or desire for revenge.

Some Poets write about Killing and Murder

The Man He Killed (Pages 16-17)

1) In this poem, a soldier talks about a man he killed during a battle. He points out the irony that if he had met the man in other circumstances, they might have been friends.
2) He imagines that the man he killed was rather like himself. He might have only enlisted in the army because he was unemployed and needed a job. Even though officially the man was his "foe", there wasn't necessarily anything bad about him.
3) The poem points out how foolish and wasteful the killing in war is: "You shoot a fellow down / You'd treat if met where any bar is".

Maybe we should just go for a pint.

The Laboratory (Pages 30-31)

1) The woman in this poem wants to kill her lover's new mistress.
2) She is obsessed by her jealousy and the idea of violent revenge. She sounds excited by the idea of killing and causing pain — "Let death be felt and the proof remain".
3) Getting the poison to kill her rival, makes the woman elated and happy. She even offers to kiss the old man who's prepared the poison.

Other Poets write about Grief and Loss

On my first Sonne (Pages 6-7)

1) The poet expresses his grief over the loss of a child: "Farewell, thou child of my right hand, and joy".
2) The poet tries to find something positive in his son's death — that at least the boy has escaped many of life's troubles and old age.
3) He pays tribute to his son, by saying he was "his best piece of poetrie" — his best work. He vows never to love anything so much again, in case he loses it.

October (Pages 62-63)

1) The poet describes a friend's funeral, one autumn.
2) The autumn weather is linked to death and grief — the "rain, weeping in the air", the wind causing a "broken branch, / a dead arm in the bright trees".
3) She describes the funeral in quite a brutal way which suggests she feels hurt by it — "My friend dead", "her short ride to the hawthorn hedge", "the earth's thud".
4) Her friend's death makes her think about her own death. It makes her "panic", but it also gives her determination that she must make the most of the life she's got left.

This topic's a bit bleak...

There are many different attitudes to death in the poems from the Anthology — sadness, acceptance, bitterness... Other poems which talk about death are: 'Tichborne's Elegy' (p.14-15), 'Ulysses' (p.26-27), 'Mid-Term Break' (p.46-47) and 'On the Train' (p.64-65).

Parent/Child Relationships

Family arguments — a valuable source of poetic inspiration.

1) The parent/child relationship is central to most people's lives.
2) Parent/child relationships often change as the people grow older.
3) Parent/child relationships often contain some conflict.

Some Children want Independence from their Parents

Catrin (Pages 52-53)

1) The poet remembers the birth of her daughter. She describes it as "our first / Fierce confrontation". The struggle for independence between mother and daughter had already begun.
2) The poet says that there is a "rope of love" pulling her and her daughter together, but at the same time they have always been struggling to be separate: "To be two, to be ourselves".
3) As her daughter asks if she can "skate / In the dark, for one more hour" the poet feels torn. She understands her daughter's urge to be independent, but at the same time she feels loving and protective of her.

Parents and Children can have very Different Characters

Ulysses (Pages 26-27)

1) The narrator of this poem is the great Greek hero Ulysses. He's old now, but still desperate for travel and adventure, "I cannot rest from travel: I will drink / Life to the lees".
2) He's bored and frustrated with living at home with his "agèd wife", ruling a "savage race" of people.
3) Ulysses describes his son, Telemachus, as having a very different character and outlook to himself. Telemachus is happy to patiently rule the island, and gradually "make mild / A rugged people".
4) When Ulysses describes Telemachus and his work he uses dull words and phrases like "slow prudence", "useful and the good", "duties" and "decent". This is in strong contrast to the vibrant way he describes himself, e.g."a hungry heart", "honoured" and "yearning in desire".

Digging (Pages 44-45)

1) The poet sees his old father digging in the garden, and this reminds him of how skilled and strong his father and grandfather used to be at digging — "By God, the old man could handle a spade".
2) The poet hasn't followed in their footsteps — he's inside writing, not outside digging. He says, "I've no spade to follow men like them".
3) At the end of the poem, he draws a parallel between digging and writing: "The squat pen rests. / I'll dig with it". He hopes to gain the same pride and strength from writing as his elders did from digging.

Most Parents Care Deeply about their Children

The Affliction of Margaret (Pages 10-11)

1) The woman in the poem hasn't heard from her son for 7 years. We see her anguish at not knowing whether her son is dead or alive — "My apprehensions come in crowds".
2) She's desperate to hear from him, whatever has happened to him: "Oh find me, prosperous or undone!".
3) She describes her son as if he's almost perfect: "He was among the prime in worth".
4) She dearly loves her son, but we don't find out how he feels about her.

Everyone starts off as a squalling baby...

Other poems which describe parent/child relationships are 'On my first Sonne' (p.6-7), 'Mali' (p.56-57), 'The Field-Mouse' (p.60-61) and 'Cold Knap Lake' (p.66-67).

Danger

Some people are scared by danger — others get a kick out of it.

1) Danger can arise from the natural environment, e.g. storms.
2) Danger can also be caused by people — through aggression and violence.
3) Sometimes a danger is just in people's imaginations — it doesn't really exist.

Danger can come from the Environment

Patrolling Barnegat (Pages 18-19)

1) The poem describes a small band of watchmen patrolling the beach during a fierce storm.
2) The storm is described as very powerful: "Waves, air, midnight, their savagest trinity lashing". It is an uncontrollable part of nature: "Wild, wild the storm".
3) The storm is dangerous — out to sea the watchmen wonder if they can see a wrecked ship: "is that a wreck? is the red signal flaring?".

The Little Boy Lost and The Little Boy Found (Pages 12-13)

1) The boy in the poems is lost in a "lonely fen".
2) The boy is helpless on his own and in danger of being hurt — "the mire was deep, and the child did weep".
3) This danger is averted when God appears, "like his father in white".
4) Blake uses the story to make a religious point — he says we're lost without God.

Danger can come from People's Violence and Aggression

The Field-Mouse (Pages 60-61)

1) In this poem, the poet worries about the violence going on in former-Yugoslavia. She dreams about a similar conflict happening in her own country and how it would affect her family.
2) She dreams that her home is part of a battleground — "the air / stammering with gunfire". In her dream, her neighbour becomes her enemy, "wounding my land with stones".
3) She's particularly frightened by how vulnerable her children would be in a conflict. She dreams they "dance in grass" as the gunfire goes on around them.

Danger can be in the Imagination

Death of a Naturalist (Pages 42-43)

1) In this poem, a boy becomes fascinated with a place where wildlife has gathered around some rotting flax in a stream. He takes frogspawn away from the dam to show at school.
2) One day, the boy goes to the dam and finds it full of frogs. He's frightened by the frogs. He thinks they're repulsive — "gross-bellied" with "loose necks".
3) The boy thinks the frogs are violent and threatening — they look like "grenades" and sound like "obscene threats". He thinks they want some kind of revenge on him, for taking away frogspawn.
4) In his fear, the boy runs away. His childish imagination believes that if he dipped his hand in the water "the spawn would clutch it". The danger in this poem is mostly in the character's imagination.

Be afraid, be very afraid...

This is a bit of a grim topic — people being frightened and getting hurt. If you want more of this doleful stuff, then read: 'Storm on the Island' (p.48-49), 'On the Train' (p.64-65) and 'Cold Knap Lake' (p.66-67).

Attitudes Towards Other People

Poems are often about the poet's attitudes and feelings towards other people. Sometimes their attitude towards others is very nice, and sometimes it's, erm, not...

1) Some poets write about positive attitudes and feelings towards other people.
2) Some poets write about negative or violent attitudes towards other people.
3) Sometimes a poet writes about conflicting or uncertain attitudes towards others.

Poems can show Positive Attitudes Towards Others

Digging (Pages 44-45)

1) The poet watches his father digging in the garden, and it reminds him of his father digging potatoes twenty years before, and his grandfather cutting turf.
2) The poet's attitude to his father and grandfather is one of pride and respect. For example, he exclaims, "By God, the old man could handle a spade. / Just like his old man". This shows that even now, looking back, he still has feelings of awe for their power and skill.
3) He says that his grandfather, "cut more turf in a day / Than any other man on Toner's bog." This sounds like he's boasting, and shows how proud he is of his grandfather.

Poems can show Negative Attitudes Towards Others

Baby-sitting (Pages 54-55)

1) In this poem, a baby-sitter describes her thoughts about the baby she is looking after.
2) Her attitude to the baby is one of fear and distrust. She describes the baby in a very cold, detached way: "she is fair; / She is a perfectly acceptable child".
3) The baby-sitter feels inadequate because she's not the baby's mother. She worries that if the baby wakes, she'll be upset her mother's not there: "If she wakes / She will hate me".

"Mad, moi?"

The Laboratory (Pages 30-31)

1) The woman in the poem has a really angry attitude towards her lover and his new mistress. She thinks they've made a fool of her: "they laugh, laugh at me".
2) She's intent on revenge and wants to use poison to kill the mistress in a painful way: "Let death be felt and the proof remain". Through killing his mistress, she hopes to hurt her lover as well: "He is sure to remember her dying face!".
3) She is excited about the idea of killing and getting revenge. She has no guilt about what she is doing.

Poems sometimes show Mixed Feelings Towards Others

The Village Schoolmaster (Pages 28-29)

1) The narrator describes the former schoolmaster of a country village. The narrator's attitude towards the schoolmaster isn't entirely positive or negative.
2) The narrator sometimes seems to mock the schoolmaster, e.g. he says that he didn't like losing an argument and would keep arguing "even though vanquished". But on the other hand, he also seems to have quite fond memories of the schoolmaster. He says he was "kind" and loved learning.
3) Overall, the narrator gives the impression that although the schoolmaster was a bit pompous, he wasn't a bad man.

Anger, resentment, love, lust, hate, jealousy, contempt...

Poems which show characters' attitudes towards other people include: 'The Song of the Old Mother' (p.8-9), 'My Last Duchess' (p.22-23), 'Catrin' (p.52-53) and 'Follower' (p.50-51).

Love

There are quite a few poems on the good old-fashioned theme of love in this anthology, but not many of them are romantic. Some of them cover love of families, love of nature etc...

1) Some poets write about romantic love.
2) Poets also write about family love, e.g. between mother and daughter.
3) Some poets write about their love of nature, or a particular place or pastime.

Some Poems are about Romantic Love

Sonnet 130 (Pages 20-21)

1) This poem is a sonnet (it's 14 lines long). Sonnet form is often used for love poetry.
2) In the first part of the poem, Shakespeare goes against the reader's expectations of a love sonnet. He's pretty rude about his mistress, e.g. he says her "eyes are nothing like the sun", her hair is like "black wires" and her breath "reeks".
3) On line 9, he says "I love to hear her speak". This is the first hint that he does love his mistress.
4) In the last two lines, the tone changes. Shakespeare declares that his mistress is just as wonderful as any woman who's praised with silly compliments: "I think my love as rare / As any she belied with false compare".

Some Poems are about Loving your Family

Mali (Pages 56-57)

1) The poet remembers her granddaughter's birth and how it made her feel.
2) The birth of her granddaughter reminded her of the birth of her own daughter: "that unmistakable brim and tug of the tide / I'd thought was over."
3) The poet felt a very strong love for her granddaughter right from the start: "I'm hooked again, life-sentenced. / Even the sea could not draw me from her".
4) There's a suggestion that the poet didn't expect to be feeling these emotions again, but that once she saw her granddaughter, she couldn't help herself.

Some Poems are about Love of Places or Nature

Sonnet (Pages 34-35)

1) The poet describes how much he loves the countryside in summer.
2) He starts three lines with the phrase "I love" which emphasises his feelings.
3) He describes the countryside in a very positive way, using words like "beaming", "happy" and "bright" to show how much he likes it.

Inversnaid (Pages 32-33)

1) The poet describes a place with wild, natural scenery, with a "darksome burn" rolling through the hills.
2) In the final stanza, the poet makes an appeal for places like this to be left alone. He loves the "wilderness" and wants it to survive.

"Who cares about boys? I love shrubbery..."

Some Poets love Wolverhampton Wanderers...

The poems in this anthology are pretty bleak — even the poems about love tend to be a bit depressing. Other poems about love include: 'On my first Sonne' (p.6-7), 'The Affliction of Margaret' (p.10-11), 'Digging' (p.44-45) and 'Catrin' (p.52-53).

Memory

Many poems are based around memories — of people, events and feelings.

1) Memories can be associated with many different feelings, e.g. pride, shame, joy or anger.
2) People sometimes block out bad memories.
3) Memories can be unreliable — you might remember things differently to how they actually happened.

The Way we Remember Things Might Not be Accurate

Cold Knap Lake (Pages 66-67)

1) The poet remembers seeing her mother resuscitate a girl who had nearly drowned in a lake.
2) The poet wonders if the memory is real: "Was I there?".
3) She describes the memory as if it is a dramatic story, with her mum as the "heroine". This makes it seem possible that the event has either been enhanced in her memory, or perhaps made up altogether.
4) The poet uses the lake as a metaphor for memory. Things get lost in the lake (and her memory) which she can't find again: "All lost things lie under closing water / in that lake with the poor man's daughter".

My Last Duchess (Pages 22-23)

1) The narrator of the poem looks at a painting of his dead wife and describes what she was like.
2) The narrator's memories of his wife are warped by his feelings of jealousy and anger.
3) He says that his wife used to smile and blush at everyone, not just him: "She had / A heart - how shall I say? - too soon made glad".
4) The narrator's pride was hurt by this. He thought his wife should devote all her attention to him, and ignore other men. He suggests she was being unfaithful — "her looks went everywhere".
5) The narrator says he "gave commands; / Then all smiles stopped together". This implies that he had his wife killed.

Some Memories inspire Pride or Affection

The Village Schoolmaster (Pages 28-29)

1) At the beginning of the poem the narrator points out where the old school was in the village and starts describing what the old schoolmaster was like. It sounds as if the school might be derelict now — "Beside yon straggling fence".
2) The narrator finds humour in his memories of the schoolmaster, which suggests he was quite fond of him, even if he didn't respect him. For example, he says the schoolmaster would never give in in an argument — "even though vanquished, he could argue still".

Ulysses (Pages 26-27)

1) Ulysses has returned to his home of Ithaca after years spent away. He finds normal life boring, and wants to return to travelling and adventure.
2) Ulysses has strong memories of the glory of his former life. He remembers the "drunk delight of battle" and all that he has "seen and known".
3) In his past life, he became famous and had an impact on events. He says, "I am a part of all that I have met".
4) He's proud of his achievements. Memories of his past glory inspire him to go travelling again — "I cannot rest from travel: I will drink / Life to the lees".

"Give me a sword and I'll show you a thing or two."

I remember it well...

Other poems which deal with memories are: 'The Affliction of Margaret' (p.10-11), 'Blackberry-Picking' (p.40-41), 'Death of a Naturalist' (p.42-43), 'Digging' (p.44-45) and 'Catrin' (p.52-53).

Politics

Politics is about how a country is run, and how a government treats its citizens.
Politics affects both society as a whole and individual people.

1) Politics can be about conflict and peacemaking.
2) Politics can be about the differences between rich and poor.
3) It can be about how leaders use and abuse their power.

Politics can be about Conflict

Storm on the Island (Pages 48-49)

1) The first eight letters of the poem's title spell Stormont. Stormont is the seat of government in Northern Ireland. It has been seen as a symbol of Unionist (pro-British) power.
2) The poem uses a lot of language associated with war and violence to describe the storm, e.g. "Blast", "strafes" and "bombarded".
3) The storm battering the island might be a metaphor for the troubles in Northern Ireland.

The Field-Mouse (Pages 60-61)

1) The poet describes spending a day cutting hay on her farm, while abroad violent events are happening in the former-Yugoslavia.
2) She tries to avoid the news. She works "at the end of the meadow, / far from the radio's terrible news" and at the end of the day she "can't face the newspapers".
3) But even so, she can't help thinking about the terrible events that are happening. A field-mouse wounded during the harvest reminds her of the innocent victims of the conflict.
4) She dreams about civil war happening in her own country — her neighbour turning against her and "wounding my land with stones".

Politics can be about Peacemaking

A Difficult Birth, Easter 1998 (Pages 58-59)

1) The title of the poem refers to the Good Friday Agreement in Easter 1998. This was a peace agreement which arranged the setting up of a new power-sharing assembly in Northern Ireland.
2) The poem uses the event of an old ewe giving birth as a metaphor for the peace talks.
3) The poet says they didn't expect the old ewe to give birth: "We thought her barren". There is a parallel with the peace talks — after such a long conflict, few people expected a happy outcome.
4) The birth is difficult and drawn-out. The poet describes helping — "We strain together, harder than we dared". This is a metaphor for how difficult the peace talks were.
5) The ewe successfully gives birth — a sign of new life and hope. This represents the peace agreement.

Politics affects Individuals

The Man He Killed (Pages 16-17)

1) A soldier talks about a man he killed in battle. He didn't have any personal reason for killing the man. He has to struggle to think of the reason he killed him: "because — / Because he was my foe".
2) The soldier imagines the other man was probably quite like him: joining up because he was poor and needed a job.
3) There's implied criticism of the governments who sent the men to war. If it hadn't been for the war, the two men could have been friends.

Politics isn't just about the government at Whitehall...

Politics affects many areas of life: education, the legal system, healthcare, welfare, defence...
The Heaney / Clarke poems in the Anthology tend to focus on politics as a source of conflict.

Getting Older

People's personalities, outlook and capabilities often change as they get older. Adolescence and old age are two important times in life which poets often write about.

1) Adolescence can be a difficult and emotional time. This is the period when people start to become independent and learn to cope with life on their own.
2) Old age can also be a difficult period of life. The approach of death can make people think about what they want from the life they've got left.

Growing up is about Becoming Independent

Catrin (Pages 52-53)

1) The poet describes how she and her daughter have always wanted independence from each other. Even the birth felt like a struggle for independence: "to become / Separate".
2) At the same time there is a strong bond between the two of them, which makes the poet very protective of her daughter: "the tight / Red rope of love".
3) As her daughter grows up, she continues the fight to be independent of her mother, asking with a "Defiant glare" if she can "skate / In the dark, for one more hour".

Growing up can be Emotional and Difficult

Blackberry-Picking (Pages 40-41)

1) This poem is about the disappointment the poet experienced during his childhood when the blackberries he picked rotted.
2) The first part of the poem describes his childish delight in the "glossy purple" blackberries. The second part shows his disappointment when they rotted: "I always felt like crying. It wasn't fair".
3) Gradually, as he grows up, he gets used to the fact that the blackberries are going to go rotten, and that good things don't always last — "Each year I hoped they'd keep, knew they would not".

They're only blackberries, Seamus.

Old Age can Motivate People to Get the Most Out of Life

Ulysses (Pages 26-27)

1) Ulysses was one of the great Greek heroes. In this poem, he has grown old and is living a quiet life on the island of Ithaca with his family. He's bored with life at home. Even though he is old he says he "cannot rest from travel", and seeks more adventure and glory.
2) Ulysses is aware that he is ageing and not as strong as he used to be, but he's defiant — "Made weak by time and fate, but strong in will".
3) He gathers his crew and encourages them to join him in one more voyage. He says that even though they are old, "Some work of noble note, may yet be done".

October (Pages 62-63)

1) The poet goes to a friend's funeral. It makes her think about her own approaching death.
2) She doesn't want to feel defeated by death. Instead she decides to keep on working and writing as much as she can: "passing my death-day, winning ground."

This page is dedicated to Adrian Mole Aged 13 and 3/4...

Other poems about growing up and growing older are: 'The Song of the Old Mother' (p.8-9), 'Follower' (p.50-51) and 'Mali' (p.56-57). That's it for poets' ideas, attitudes and feelings. Phew.

Strong Emotions

Poets often show strong emotions in their poems — either their own emotions, or those of the people they are writing about. Strong emotions are things like love, hate, anger, jealousy and joy.

1) Poems are often about personal subjects, which the poet feels strong emotions about.
2) Poems about difficult situations often contain strong emotions, e.g. poems about death or danger.
3) Poets can show strong emotions through the language they use to write about a subject.
4) When a poet writes about strong emotions, it can make the reader think about times when they felt the same way. It often increases the connection the reader feels to the poem.

Poems about Difficult Situations show Strong Emotions

Mid-Term Break (Pages 46-47)

1) The poet describes going home from boarding school for his young brother's funeral.
2) He describes his father crying, even though in the past "He had always taken funerals in his stride".
3) His mother doesn't cry — she puts on a brave front for the "strangers" at the house. But her "coughed out angry tearless sighs" and the way she holds her son's hand, show how upset she is.
4) The language the poet uses to describe his brother's corpse is very simple and effective. It shows the grief and shock he feels.
5) He says his brother lay in his coffin, "as in his cot" — the contrast between a living boy in a cot, and a corpse in a coffin is shocking and very sad. The final line, "A four foot box, a foot for every year" also emphasises how young his brother was when he died.

Tichborne's Elegy (Pages 14-15)

1) This poem was written as the poet was waiting for his execution in the Tower of London.
2) The poet feels huge sadness and bitterness about his coming execution.
3) Throughout the poem, he keeps pointing out the bitter irony of his situation: even though he is young and healthy, his life is coming to an end: "My fruit is fallen, and yet my leaves are green".
4) He feels angry about the way his life is going to be wasted. Instead of being able to enjoy his life, it's going to be cut short: "My prime of youth is but a frost of cares".

On the Train (Pages 64-65)

1) The poet is travelling home on a train, as news comes through about a terrible train crash. She describes the crash as a "blazing bone-ship" which is a terrifying image.
2) She describes the pain of the relatives and friends of those killed in the crash. She imagines them trying to phone their loved ones and getting no answer — the "wolves howl into silent telephones".
3) The news of the crash makes the poet anxious to contact her own home and let her partner know she's safe.

Poets often write about things they're Passionate about

Inversnaid (Pages 32-33)

1) This poem is about a place in the countryside which the poet really loves, where a "darksome burn" rolls through the hills.
2) In the last stanza, the poet makes an impassioned plea for places like this to be left as they are: "What would the world be, once bereft / Of wet and of wildness? Let them be left".

Strong emotions are dramatic and compelling...

Poems are often about personal or dramatic events — no wonder they're emotional. 'On my first Sonne' (p.6-7) and 'The Field-Mouse' (p.60-61) are also good examples of this theme.

Use of First Person

If the poet writes in the first person, they use words like "I" and "me", rather than "she" and "him".

1) Writing in the first person allows the poet to use their voice directly.
2) This allows them to talk about their personal thoughts and emotions.
3) The first person lets us see things from the poet or character's point of view.

Writing in the First Person can Express Personal Feelings

Baby-sitting (Pages 54-55)

1) This poem is about a baby-sitter's negative feelings towards the baby she is looking after.
2) The use of the first person means we hear the babysitter's thoughts directly. This gives her thoughts and feelings more impact.
3) Simple statements like "I don't love / This baby" and "I am afraid of her" are shocking because they are the opposite of how people usually think about children.

Sonnet (Pages 34-35)

1) This poem is about how much the poet loves the countryside in summer.
2) Three lines of the poem start with "I love" which emphasises his feelings.

Digging (Pages 44-45)

1) The poet describes watching his father digging the garden and the feelings and thoughts this provokes. We hear his thoughts directly because he's writing in the first person.
2) He feels pride in his father and grandfather's skill at digging, and guilt that he hasn't followed their way of life — "I've no spade to follow men like them".
3) At the end of the poem, he finds a resolution to this problem. He will follow his father and grandfather in spirit, but using his writer's pen as his tool, instead of a spade.

Writing in the First Person can be Persuasive

The Man He Killed (Pages 16-17)

1) This poem makes a point about the barbarity and foolishness of war — how people who could be friends kill each other because they are on different sides.
2) Hardy writes in the first person from the point of view of a soldier who has fought in a war. This increases the impact of the message, because the character is speaking from personal experience.
3) Using the first person makes it sound as if the character is talking directly to the reader: "I shot him dead because — / Because he was my foe". This makes the poem more compelling and persuasive.

The Song of the Old Mother (Pages 8-9)

1) The message of the poem is about how harsh life is for many old people.
2) The poet writes in the first person, from the point of view of an old cleaning woman.
3) The character of the cleaning woman talks directly to the reader about her situation. She describes her list of chores, starting early "in the dawn" and not stopping till the "stars" are out. She contrasts this with the "idleness" of young people.
4) The poem gives a voice to a character who would usually be ignored.

The first person lets the poet speak directly to the reader...

'Tichborne's Elegy' (p.14-15) and 'On the Train' (p.64-65) also use the first person. It makes a big difference to the effect of a poem, as it lets the poet talk personally — poems like 'The Man He Killed' would lose a lot of impact if it was just "he" or "she" instead of "I".

Characters

Most poets write about people — apart from the nature-loving, obsessed-with-potatoes brigade.

1) Many poems are about a particular character — their personality, actions and emotions.
2) The characters in a poem can be real or completely made-up.
3) Sometimes the main character is the poet themselves.
4) Often an important character isn't actually present in the poem — they're just talked about by the other characters.

The Poet has an Opinion about the Characters

Catrin (Pages 52-53)

1) The poet describes her daughter, Catrin, as a strong character, wanting independence from her mother, e.g. she demands to be allowed to stay out late "In the dark, for one more hour".
2) The poet seems to have a difficult relationship with her daughter. She describes the birth as "our first / Fierce confrontation" — suggesting it was the first of many.
3) The poet describes her daughter as beautiful — "your straight, strong, long / Brown hair". But even this admiration is mixed with feelings of conflict — "your rosy, / Defiant glare".

Another poem about his Dad. What about me, huh?

Follower (Pages 50-51)

1) The poem is about the poet's relationship with his father.
2) The poet describes being a child following his father around the farm. He admired his father's strength and skill: "The horses strained at his clicking tongue. / An expert".
3) Now they are both older, their relationship is reversed: "today / It is my father who keeps stumbling / Behind me". The poet's view of his father has changed.

Sometimes a Key Character is Absent

The Affliction of Margaret (Pages 10-11)

1) In this poem, a woman called Margaret worries about what has happened to her son who disappeared seven years ago. Even though we never meet the son, he is an important character in the poem.
2) Margaret's opinion of her son is very warm and positive. She says that he was "among the prime in worth, / An object beauteous to behold".
3) There are hints though, that her son wasn't perfect. She says, "If things ensued that wanted grace, / As hath been said, they were not base". This suggests that other people didn't like his behaviour — but Margaret still defends him.
4) The fact that he's left his mother without word for seven years, suggests he might not care about her. The sadness of the poem comes from the fact that she still cares so much for him.

My Last Duchess (Pages 22-23)

1) In the poem, a rich man looks at a painting of his dead wife, and describes what she was like.
2) The character of the dead wife is described in a lot of detail — but all through the eyes of her husband, who didn't trust her. We never hear her side of the story.
3) The husband says his wife made him angry because she favoured everyone with her smiles and blushes, rather than saving them for him. There is a suggestion that she was unfaithful to him: "she liked whate'er / She looked on, and her looks were everywhere."

Characters are just the people in a poem...

Other poems with strong characters include: 'The Song of the Old Mother' (p.8-9), 'The Village Schoolmaster' (p.28-29), 'The Laboratory' (p.30-31) and 'Death of a Naturalist' (p.42-43).

Imagery

The way a poet writes can make you form a picture in your head of what's being described — this is called "imagery". Two common forms of imagery are metaphors and similes (see glossary).

1) Imagery helps the reader imagine the situations, characters and emotions described in a poem.
2) Imagery often uses comparisons to describe something, e.g. "She ran like the wind".

Some Images Appeal to our Emotions

The Field-Mouse (Pages 60-61)

1) In this poem, the poet spends the day cutting hay with her family, and worries about the violence going on abroad, in former-Yugoslavia.
2) The poet uses war-like language to describe the hay-cutting: "killed flowers", "the field lies bleeding", "the field's hurt". This imagery links the hay-cutting to the violence going on abroad.
3) She describes a "quivering mouse" hurt during the harvest, which dies in her child's hands. This image is very moving: "It curls in agony big as itself / and the star goes out in its eye".
4) She then dreams about her own children in a situation as violent as that in former-Yugoslavia. She describes them as being as vulnerable and breakable as the field-mouse: "their bones brittle as mouse-ribs".

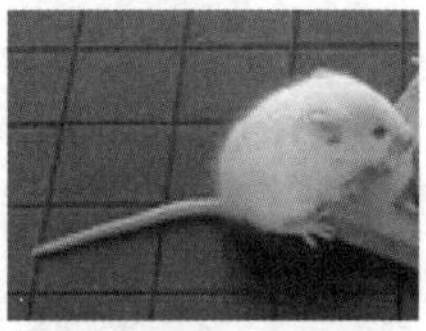
The rarely spotted metaphor-mouse

At a Potato Digging (Pages 36-37)

1) This poem describes both a modern-day potato digging, and the Irish potato famine in the 1840s.
2) Bleak imagery is used to describe the potato digging — the "ragged" line of people are like "crows attacking" the fields.
3) Religious imagery is also used to describe the digging — "Processional stooping through the turf". This emphasises how important the potato crop is. Without it, there is the threat of famine.
4) Shocking imagery is used to describe the starving people during the famine — "Mouths tightened in".

Poets use Imagery to Describe Places

Patrolling Barnegat (Pages 18-19)

1) The poet describes watchmen patrolling the beach during a fierce storm. He uses imagery to create a sense of how strong and frightening the storm is.
2) He describes the bad weather as if it is a violent, attacking force — e.g. "savagest trinity lashing".
3) The sound of the gale is described as if it's a person's voice: there's an "incessant undertone muttering" and sometimes it sounds like someone shrieking with "demoniac laughter".
4) He emphasises the gloominess of the scene with words like "midnight", "shadows" and "murk".

Inversnaid (Pages 32-33)

1) The poet describes a place he loves in the countryside. He makes an appeal for wild, natural places to be left as they are.
2) He builds up an image of the "darksome burn" in the first three verses. He emphasises the colours: the river is "horseback brown", the lake "pitchblack" and the froth on the lake "fawn".
3) He also describes the movement of the place: the river "roaring down" to the lake, the froth "Turns and twindles" over the water and the brook "treads through" the hills.

Imagery is an important poetic device...

Most poems have a bit of imagery in. Examples you can look at include: 'Tichborne's Elegy' (p.14-15), 'Ulysses' (p.26-27), 'Sonnet' (p.34-35), 'Perch' (p.38-39), 'Death of a Naturalist' (p.42-43), 'Mali' (p.56-57), 'October (p.62-63) and 'On the Train' (p.64-65).

Closing Couplets

A closing couplet is the last two lines of a poem.

1) A closing couplet can sum up the poem as a whole.
2) A closing couplet can make a new or surprising point, giving the poem an unexpected conclusion.
3) Closing couplets can be set apart from the rest of the poem, and sometimes they rhyme.

Closing Couplets can Sum Up a Poem

Cold Knap Lake (Pages 66-67)

1) The closing couplet sums up the main issue of the poem.
2) The first 14 lines describe an incident she remembers from her childhood, when her mother saved a drowning girl from a lake. Then the poet wonders whether this really happened or not.
3) The last two lines say that we can't be sure whether distant memories are real or not — "All lost things lie under closing water".
4) This is the only rhyming couplet of the poem, bringing it to a neat conclusion.

Storm on the Island (Pages 48-49)

1) The poem describes the inhabitants of an island preparing for a great storm. There is no shelter on the island, and their houses are battered by the strong wind.
2) The final two lines sum up the idea of how strong and frightening the wind is even though it's invisible — "We are bombarded by the empty air".
3) The poet is quite philosophical in the final line: "Strange, it is a huge nothing that we fear".

And still the wonder grew.

The Village Schoolmaster (Pages 28-29)

1) The closing couplet seems to sum up the poem, by telling us how the villagers were baffled by how much the schoolmaster knew.
2) There is some uncertainty too. The phrase "and still the wonder grew" could mean that the villagers are impressed by the schoolmaster — but it also suggests that they found him strange.

Closing Couplets can be Surprising

Sonnet 130 (Pages 20-21)

1) Shakespeare seems to be criticising his mistress, but the last two lines show he does love her really.
2) The closing couplet surprises the reader. It makes us look at the rest of the poem in a different way.
3) His love seems all the more genuine because he knows she's not perfect — "I think my love as rare / As any she belied with false compare".

Follower (Pages 50-51)

1) The poet describes being a child, following his father around the farm. His father was strong and skilful and the poet looked up to him.
2) In the last two lines this situation is reversed. Now it is his father "who keeps stumbling / Behind me and will not go away".

Closing couplets leave a lasting impression on the reader...

This is a tricky theme to write an essay on. Think about what the closing two lines add to the poem. Other poems with interesting closing couplets are: 'The Song of the Old Mother (p.8-9), 'Inversnaid' (p.32-33), 'A Difficult Birth, Easter 1998' (p.58-59) and 'October' (p.62-63).

Irony

Irony can be funny, but it can also be tragic.

1) It's ironic when words are used in a sarcastic or comic way to imply the opposite of what they normally mean. People often do this to draw attention to something being funny or odd.
2) It's ironic when there is a big difference between what people expect or hope for and what actually happens.

Sometimes the Whole Poem is Ironic

Tichborne's Elegy (Pages 14-15)

1) The irony in this poem is that even though the poet is still young and healthy, his life is almost over because he is about to be executed: "My youth is spent, and yet I am not old".
2) Tichborne repeats this idea throughout the poem, with each line making clear the bitter irony of his situation: "And now I live, and now my life is done".

The Village Schoolmaster (Pages 28-29)

1) The poet uses irony in his description of the schoolmaster. He uses it to show how the schoolmaster was a bit pretentious and pompous.
2) He says things which sound at first like they're praise, but turn out to be pretty sarcastic. For example, he says that the schoolmaster was skilful at arguing, but then says this is because he'd never stop "even though vanquished". He also says the schoolmaster had "many a joke" but suggests these weren't funny, because the children had to pretend to laugh at them.
3) The poet implies that the "rustics" found the schoolmaster impressive because they didn't understand him. The things he said sounded good ("words of learned length and thundering sound") and so they assumed he must be really clever.

The Man He Killed (Pages 16-17)

1) The poet points out that the man he shot dead could have been his friend if they'd met in different circumstances.
2) It's ironic that, if they'd met "By some old ancient inn", rather than being lined up against each other across a battlefield, they would have been having a drink together instead of shooting at each other.
3) The irony in this poem is pretty bitter, for example when the narrator says "Yes; quaint and curious war is!". Although the poem uses irony, it's making a serious point about the waste and tragedy of war.

Irony Can Come Out at the End of the Poem

Follower (Pages 50-51)

1) The poet describes how he followed his father, the "expert" in ploughing.
2) The poet "stumbled in his hob-nailed wake" — he greatly respected his father and wanted to be like him.
3) At the end, the roles are reversed — "It is my father who keeps stumbling / Behind me". Ironically, his father, who he had always worshipped, is now a nuisance following him.

Isn't it ironic...

Other poems with a spot of irony include: 'Sonnet 130' (p.20-21), 'My Last Duchess' (p.22-23) and 'Death of a Naturalist' (p.42-43).

Language Effects

Language effects are the way the sounds of words in a poem are used to make a certain impression on the reader. Examples of language effects are alliteration, rhyme, assonance and onomatopoeia.

1) Language effects can create a mood or atmosphere in a poem.
2) Language effects can be useful for creating a vivid picture in the reader's mind of the place or person described in the poem.
3) Language effects can make a poet's feelings or opinions more forceful and convincing.

Language Effects Can be Used to Describe Nature

Perch (Pages 38-39)

1) The alliteration in "runty and ready" reinforces the small but lively impression we get of the perch.
2) Assonance of the words "grunts", "runty" and "bluntly" drives home the ordinary appearance of the fish.

Inversnaid (Pages 32-33)

1) Alliteration in the phrase "rollrock highroad roaring" makes the reader think of the roar of the water flowing down over the stony bed of the stream.
2) The harsh alliteration of "In coop and in comb" add to the impression of a rugged setting.
3) Rhyming couplets and a regular rhythm give the poem a natural and attractive feel.
4) In the last verse, the poet makes a point about how important it is to keep places like Inversnaid as they are. Repeating "w" sounds makes the poet's point more effectively, by reminding us of the sounds of the countryside, like the wind blowing around the hills.

Language Effects make Descriptions seem More Vivid

On the Train (Pages 64-65)

1) In the first four lines, alliteration suggests the rhythm of the train journey: "flooded fields", "rocking, rocking the rails", "black box", and "tea trembles".
2) In the last stanza, the poet uses short sentences and a direct question to show her anxiety: "I phone. No answer. Where are you now?".

At a Potato Digging (Pages 36-37)

1) Heaney uses alliteration to make his descriptions more vivid. For example, alliteration in the phrases "A higgledy line from hedge to headland" and "ragged ranks" creates an image of the potato diggers as a scattered band of people working together.
2) The poem also uses repetition of distinctive words to link different parts of the poem. For example, the line of modern-day potato diggers is described as "higgledy". Later in the poem, the starved bodies of the famine victims are described as "higgledy skeletons".

Language effects make descriptions more memorable...

Learn how to spell "alliteration" before your exam. And look in the glossary to find out what assonance is, if you can't remember. Other poems which use lots of language effects are: 'Patrolling Barnegat' (p.18-19), 'The Eagle' (p.24-25) and 'Sonnet' (p.34-35).

Stage 1 — Planning

Before you write the essay, you've got to plan it. Spend ten minutes planning — that leaves you with fifty minutes for writing. Use this two-stage method to plan your essay:

A Read the Question Carefully and Underline Key Words

1) Read the question you've chosen a couple of times. The question will usually ask you how the poems show/present/use/convey the theme. Underline the theme and any other important words.
2) You have to compare four poems altogether. The question will give you the titles of one or two poems that you have to write about. You'll get some choice about which other poems you're going to compare. Pick poems which relate to the theme in the question.
3) Look up the poems you're going to write about in the copy of the Anthology you are given in the exam. Bend the corner over on those pages, so that you can find them again quickly.

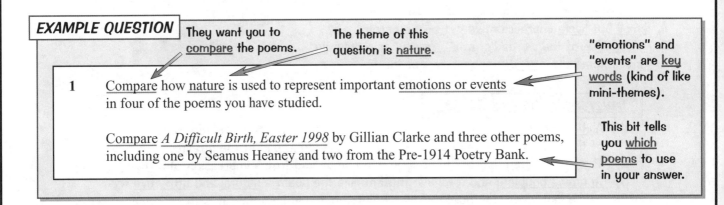

EXAMPLE QUESTION

1 Compare how nature is used to represent important emotions or events in four of the poems you have studied.

Compare *A Difficult Birth, Easter 1998* by Gillian Clarke and three other poems, including one by Seamus Heaney and two from the Pre-1914 Poetry Bank.

They want you to compare the poems.

The theme of this question is nature.

"emotions" and "events" are key words (kind of like mini-themes).

This bit tells you which poems to use in your answer.

B Spend 5-10 minutes Planning your Essay

Write a plan at the top of your answer paper — this will help you write a good essay. Just scribble stuff down, like in the example below. At the end of the exam, draw a neat line through your plan, so the examiner knows that it's rough work. Here's an example:

Plan: poems to write about: Blackberry-Picking, A Difficult Birth, Little Boy Lost, Tichborne's Elegy

1) Intro about theme - nature

2) Structure
Blackb-p: 1st stanza — joy in nature, 2nd — rot, cries
Birth: 4 verses, each about diff stage of birth/peace talks
Little boy: sad/happy halves
Tich: contrasts healthy nature / dead nature

3) Language
Black: vivid / sensory descriptions nature
Birth: descriptive details of birth
Little: sadness/loneliness of nature
Tich: metaphor nature dying/his death

4) Attitudes and Feelings
Black: joy, disappointment
Birth: tension, relief
Little: fear, wonder
Tich: sadness, injustice

5) Conclusion - personal response:
I find Tich's Elegy very moving + effective

Planning is the basis of a good essay...

Always write a plan. It'll help you get your ideas in order, and write a well-structured essay. Once you've got a plan, you know what you're going to write — it will give you confidence.

Stage 2 — Writing

Now you've planned your essay, you've got to write it.
Follow this five-step method for a brilliant essay every time.

For advice about two-part questions, see pages 86-87.

1 Write about the Theme in the Introduction

1) Get right in there — give a short definition of the theme. You don't have to go into much detail — just describe what you think the theme means.
2) Explain how the theme is explored in the poems you will write about.

2 Compare the Structures of Each Poem

1) Say how the structures of the poems relate to the theme of the question. For ideas, look at the 'What Happens in the Poem' parts of the pages on each poem.
2) Write about the similarities and differences between the structures of the poems.
3) You could write about some of these things, if any of them really stand out:

• *Line length*	• *Rhyme*	• *Rhythm*	• *Punctuation*
• *Stanza shape*	• *Repetition*	• *Narrative or time-scale*	• *Layout*

3 Compare the Use of Language in the Poems

1) Write about how the language of the poems relates to the theme of the question. For ideas, look at the 'Types of Language' parts of the pages on each poem.
2) Write about the similarities and differences in the way language is used in the poems.
3) You could write about some of these things, if any of them really stand out:

• *Images, similes and metaphors*	• *Onomatopoeia*	• *Personification*
• *Who is speaking*	• *Alliteration*	• *Mood*

Look in the glossary on pages 92-93 if you're not sure what any of these words mean.

4 Compare the Feelings and Attitudes in the Poems

1) Write about how these feelings and attitudes relate to the theme. For ideas, look at the 'Feeling and Attitudes' parts of the pages on each poem.
2) Write about the similarities and differences between the feelings and attitudes in the poems.

5 Give a Personal Response to the Poems in the Conclusion

1) Say which poem you preferred and why.
2) Show some empathy — connect the poem to your own feelings and experiences.

And finally — don't forget to check through your work...

We've included some 'A' grade essay answers on the next few pages. They use the method described here and should give you a good idea of what you're aiming for...

Sample Essay — Nature

Here's a sample 'A' grade answer to the exam question on page 84.

1 Introduction

Nature includes plants and wildlife, the weather and landscape. It is the background of much human experience and is often used by poets to represent emotions and events. In 'Blackberry-Picking' Seamus Heaney uses nature to remind us of childhood, as well as to suggest the emotions of growing up. In 'A Difficult Birth, Easter 1998', Gillian Clarke uses the story of an old ewe giving birth to represent the Irish peace talks going on at the same time. Some pre-1914 poets also use the power of nature to represent important emotions or events. William Blake uses nature to emphasise the fear of the little boy in 'The Little Boy Lost / The Little Boy Found', and Chidiock Tichborne, in 'Tichborne's Elegy' uses nature to explain the emotions he feels at the end of his life.

Start by explaining what the theme is.

Say how the theme relates to each of the poems you are writing about.

2 Structure

The way the poets structure their poems relates to their use of nature in representing emotions and events. For example, in 'Blackberry-Picking' the first stanza is about the enjoyment the children got from picking the blackberries, but in contrast, the second stanza is about their disappointment when the blackberries rotted. Similarly, in 'A Difficult Birth', each stanza shows a different stage of the birth and peace process; for example, in the third stanza, "the lamb won't come" and there seem to be difficulties, then in the fourth, the poet says "We strain together", and the lamb is born. This allows us to see the difficulty of this natural event, and gives us an idea of how difficult the peace talks were.

You've got to say how the structure of the poems relates to the theme.

Some of the pre-1914 poets also structure their poems in a way which relates to the theme. For example, William Blake has split his story about the lost boy into two short poems. In the first poem, Blake makes nature sound dangerous and frightening. There is a suggestion that the lost boy might die: "The mire was deep, and the child did weep". In the second poem, the dangers of nature are conquered by "God, ever nigh", who saves the boy and returns him to his parents. Chidiock Tichborne uses structure in a different way. In 'Tichborne's Elegy', he phrases many of the lines in repetitive way which contrasts images of health and death. Many of these images are from nature, for example: "My fruit is fallen, and yet my leaves are green".

Keep mentioning the key words in your answer — they're highlighted green in this essay.

3 Language

All four poets use language and imagery from nature to make the emotions and events in the poems seem more vivid. In 'Blackberry-Picking', Heaney uses rich, sensory language to describe the ripe blackberries, for example: "glossy purple clot", and "Like thickened wine". These descriptions help the reader imagine the look, taste and texture of the blackberries and understand the poet's emotions of hunger and "lust" for them. The language in 'A Difficult Birth' is equally descriptive. The "slippery head" of the lamb brings home the natural details of the birth, and also suggests how difficult it was to finalise the peace agreement.

Compare the way the poets have used language to present the theme.

In 'The Little Boy Lost' / 'The Little Boy Found' nature inspires the emotions of fear and loneliness in the little boy. Words like "lonely", "dark", and "vapour" create a bleak image of the mire. The boy seems at the mercy of nature, with no person to protect him: "no father was there." Tichborne also uses nature to create bleak imagery, which represents the emotions of sadness and injustice he is feeling about his imminent execution. In the first stanza, he presents images of happiness and then undermines them with contrasting images of death and decay. For example, in the line "My crop of corn is but a field of tares", the corn represents his present youth and health, and the tares (weeds) represent his future.

Back up your points with quotes from the poems.

4 Attitudes

The poets are all trying to express different feelings and attitudes through their poems and their use of images from nature. Heaney uses the story of the blackberry picking to explain his emotions of joy and disappointment when growing up and learning that though life can be "sweet", it isn't always "fair". In 'A Difficult Birth', we are taken through first tension and then relief as "he comes / in a syrupy flood". Our concern for the ewe and lamb echoes the emotions people were feeling as the peace talks dragged on. Blake uses bleak images of nature to demonstrate the fear of the little boy and his parents: for example the mother walking "in sorrow pale, through the lonely dale". Tichborne also uses images from nature to present negative emotions: fear, sadness and a sense of injustice at his fate: "The day is past, and yet I saw no sun".

Link the feelings and attitudes in the poem to the theme.

5 Conc.

In conclusion, these poems are all made more powerful through their use of nature. Natural images are used to help us imagine feelings and ideas more clearly, even if they are outside our experience. I find the use of nature to represent emotions particularly moving in 'Tichborne's Elegy' because it enables the poet to describe his feelings of sadness and pain in a very elegant way.

Include your personal response in the conclusion.

Section Six — How to Answer the Question

Sample Essay — Death

Here's another example of a typical exam question — and how to answer it well...

A Here's an Exam-style Question about Death

Question 1 You should answer both (a) and (b).

(a) Compare how death is presented in *On my first Sonne* by Ben Jonson and one other poem from the Pre-1914 Poetry Bank.

(b) Compare how death is presented in one poem by Seamus Heaney and one poem by Gillian Clarke.

B Here's an Example of a Plan for this Answer

Plan: poems to write about: On my first Sonne, The Laboratory, Mid-Term Break, October

(a) 1) Intro - death
2) Structure
Sonne: one verse, like inscription on tombstone
Laboratory: long, 12 stanzas, scattered thoughts
3) Language
Sonne: sad, proud
Lab: melodramatic, excited
4) Attitudes and feelings
Sonne: devastated but grateful - philosophical
Lab: revenge, evil
5) Conclusion
Strong contrast

(b) 1) Intro about theme - death
2) Structure
Mid-Term: last line on its own for emphasis
October: verses mark diff feelings
3) Language
Mid-Term: functional, graphic
October: harsh at first, becomes more metaphorical
4) Attitudes and feelings
Mid-Term: sadness, confusion
October: fear, determination
5) Conclusion
October has more positive message

Here's an 'A' Grade Answer to the Question

1 Intro.

(a) The poems 'On my first Sonne' and 'The Laboratory' present death in different ways. In 'On my first Sonne', the poet pays tribute to his son, who died at just seven years old. In 'The Laboratory', a lady talks to an apothecary who is preparing poison for her. She is planning murder, possibly of her lover's new mistress.

Treat each part of the question, (a) and (b), like a mini-essay.

2 Structure

The structure of the poems relates to how death is presented. 'On my first Sonne' has a simple structure, consisting of just one verse of six rhyming couplets. This creates a sense that the poem is like an inscription on a tombstone, a final fond goodbye to the poet's "lov'd boy", who has just died. In contrast, in 'The Laboratory', there are numerous stanzas. These help to represent the character's excitable, easily distracted frame of mind as she prepares for the murder.

Remember to relate the structure of the poems to the theme.

3 Language

The poets also use language very differently to present death. The woman in 'The Laboratory' describes death in a cruelly melodramatic way: "He is sure to remember her dying face!". She asks the apothecary lots of questions ("Quick—is it finished?"), which makes her appear excited about the crime. Jonson's language, on the other hand, is gentle and tender, with phrases such as "thou child of my right hand" showing the poet's love for his dead son.

The key words in the question are highlighted in green.

4 Att.

The attitudes to death contrast greatly between the two poems. Jonson is devastated by his son's death, but he says that death may actually be a better state to be in than life. He asks why people are sad about death, as dead people "have so

Give examples and quotes from the poems to back up your points.

THIS IS A FLAP. FOLD THIS PAGE OUT.

Sample Essay — Death

4 Attitudes

soone scap'd worlds, and fleshes rage". The woman in 'The Laboratory' also has a positive view of death, but her motives are much more sinister; she is excited by the thought of getting her revenge and causing pain: "Let death be felt". It gives her a sense of power over the people she imagines "laugh" at her.

Write about similarities and differences between the poems.

5 Conc.

In conclusion, there is a strong contrast in the way these two poems present death. 'On my first Sonne' is a moving poem which makes us question conventional attitudes to death by saying that death can be merciful. On the other hand, 'The Laboratory' shows a malicious, vengeful view of death. I find the descriptions of the poisons and "faint smokes curling" oppressive and smothering.

Include a conclusion for part (a).

1 Intro.

(b) Death is an emotional subject, often connected to feelings of grief, sadness and loss. In the poem 'Mid-Term Break', the poet, Seamus Heaney, talks about the funeral of his younger brother and the effects of his death on him and other members of his family. Gillian Clarke's poem 'October' also involves a funeral, but in Clarke's case, it makes her think about her own death.

Try and write a similar amount about each poem — this will make sure your answer is balanced.

2 Structure

'Mid-Term Break' is made up of seven verses of three lines each, then one line on its own at the end: "A four foot box, a foot for every year". This places the emphasis on this tragic final line, underlining how young the boy was when he died. In contrast, 'October' has a fairly irregular structure. It consists of three verses of similar but not identical length, and is written in iambic pentameter. This divides the poem into different ideas about death: in the first, death is only hinted at by images of nature; in the second, the funeral of the poet's friend is described; the third verse is about her thoughts on how she intends to "write like the wind" before she dies, giving a positive and purposeful end to an otherwise low-spirited poem.

Spend roughly half your time on (a) and half your time on (b).

3 Language

The style of language used in these poems affects the impressions of death that they give. In 'Mid-Term Break', the language has a functional but graphic feel. Apparently emotionless phrases like "In the porch I met my father crying" show that the poet remembers the funeral clearly, but, because he was only a child, was confused and didn't know what to make of it.

The style of language in 'October' is generally more emotive than that of 'Mid-Term Break'. Harsh, depressing words such as "dead", "stony" and "weeping", show the grief the poet feels for her dead friend. The third verse, however, has an urgent, hurried feel, with words like "racing" and "running" expressing the poet's recognition that she must make the most out of life before her own death.

Explain how the quotes you use help back up the point you're making.

4 Feelings and Attitudes

These two poems deal with different kinds of feelings and attitudes towards death. In 'Mid-Term Break', the poet seems saddened but also confused by his brother's death, although he rarely says how he feels, possibly because he is too young to understand what is happening. He says he felt "embarrassed / By old men standing up to shake my hand" — he seems uncomfortable rather than grief-stricken by what is happening.

If possible, work quotes into your sentences.

'October', on the other hand, contains more intense and straightforward feelings. The poet is very upset at her friend's funeral, describing "our faces / stony, rain, weeping in the air." As an adult, she has a better understanding of death, and the "panic" she feels when she thinks about her own death leads to her determination to write as much as she can while she is still alive.

5 Conc.

Both these poems contain some interesting ideas about death. I find "October" particularly interesting because the poet manages to take something positive out of her grief and fear, finishing by saying that she is "winning ground", in the race against death.

Say what your feelings about the poems are in the conclusion.

Sample Essay — Imagery

Some of the exam questions will be about poetic methods e.g. imagery, first person, character. Don't be scared off by these questions — you can still answer them by looking at the structure, language and feelings / attitudes in the poems.

A Here's an Exam-style Question about Imagery

Question 1 Compare how imagery is used to create vivid descriptions in *At a Potato Digging* by Seamus Heaney and one poem by Gillian Clarke. Then go on to compare the ways imagery is used in two of the poems from the Pre-1914 Poetry Bank.

B Here's an Example of a Plan for this Answer

Plan: poems to write about: At a Potato Digging, The Field-Mouse, Sonnet, The Eagle

1) Intro about theme - imagery

2) Structure

Potato: 4 sections about diff aspects of potato

Mouse: 3 verses - harvest, mouse, nightmare

3) Language

Potato: harsh/shocking, religious

Mouse: violent, vivid

4) Attitudes and Feelings

Potato: pain, determination

Mouse: message about war

then go on to compare pre1914 poems:

5) Structure

Sonnet: sonnet form, rhyme, repetition 'I love'

Eagle: short, rhythm, rhyme

6) Language

Sonnet: colour / shine, detailed description

Eagle: simile 'thunderbolt', image power/height

7) Attitudes and Feelings

Sonnet: joy, happiness in small things

Eagle: power, respect for nature

8) Conclusion for whole essay

Preferred Potato Digging

Here's an 'A' Grade Answer to the Question

1 Intro.

Imagery is the way poets use language to create vivid descriptions of situations, events and even emotions. Heaney's poem 'At a Potato Digging' employs some striking images of people digging potatoes up, and the potato famine of the past, while 'The Field-Mouse' by Gillian Clarke uses imagery of a harvest to represent the war in the former-Yugoslavia.

Briefly introduce the theme.

2 Structure

'At a Potato Digging' is split into four main sections, and each of these describes different images related to the theme of potatoes: workers digging potatoes today, the potatoes themselves, the potato famine, and modern workers taking a break. This structure allows us to link together the imagery of the different times. 'The Field-Mouse' has three verses, the first having sleepy images of the harvest, the second about a mouse wounded by the hay cutting, and the third, with the most vivid imagery, related to the war and the narrator's nightmare. As in 'At a Potato Digging', seemingly separate events are linked together, with the news of the war providing the background to the harvest.

This question asks for the Heaney / Clarke poems to be compared first.

Both poems use very harsh language to create vivid images. In 'At a Potato Digging', the phrase "live skulls" refers first to the potatoes, but then, more shockingly,

Back up your points with quotes.

Sample Essay — Imagery

Language 3

to the starving people during the famine. This poem also uses religious imagery to show how much people today value the potatoes — the soil is seen as "a seasonal altar". The imagery in 'The Field-Mouse' is more violent. As they cut the hay, we are told that "its wave breaks before the tractor blade", which suggests the destruction going on in Europe. Then the mouse is described; it "curls in agony big as itself", which is a small but poignant reminder of the victims of war. In the final verse, the narrator dreams of her neighbour "wounding my land with stones", and this is a very vivid description of civil war.

Compare the poets' use of language.

Feelings / Attitudes 4

The feelings suggested by the imagery in these poems are quite different. In 'At a Potato Digging', the pain and desperation of starvation is shown graphically. However, there is a sense of the modern day diggers' determination to survive. They still have a tough life, but the "higgledy line from hedge to headland" that they form shows how they admirably pull together. 'The Field-Mouse', on the other hand, contains a bleak message about the devastation caused by war. The poet describes how "the field lies bleeding" after the harvest, and the image of her neighbour attacking her family reminds us of the terrible things that humans are capable of.

Talk about how the poets use the theme to show feelings and attitudes.

Structure 5

The second part of this essay will compare the use of imagery in two pre-1914 poems: 'The Eagle' and 'Sonnet'. The structure of these poems relates to their use of imagery. 'The Eagle' is a very short poem, describing a single, striking image of an eagle perched on a crag before swooping on its prey. In a similar way, 'Sonnet' is quite a short poem with a single subject being described: the beauty of summer.

Language 6

The imagery used in the 'The Eagle' emphasises the bird's power and authority. The eagle is described as high up, looking down on the world from his "mountain walls": even the sea seems small and insignificant ("wrinkled") from his perch. The bird is described as almost human: he has "crookèd hands" not talons. The simile of a "thunderbolt" is used to describe the awe-inspiring force of the bird as it swoops for prey. In 'Sonnet' John Clare also uses imagery to describe the beauty of nature. However, he focuses on a tamer, softer side of nature: "wild flowers", "wool sack clouds" and "hay grass". He uses language to create an image of happiness: "beaming forth", "sport about", "happy wings", "play". In both poems, colour is used to accentuate the beauty of the scene: the "azure" sea in 'The Eagle' and "stain with gold" in 'Sonnet'.

Be careful to leave time to write about all four poems.

Explain the methods the poet has used to create an overall image.

Attitudes 7

The imagery Tennyson uses in 'The Eagle' shows his feelings of respect for nature and the beauty of the world. He describes a natural environment of sea, cliffs and sun, untouched by humans. 'Sonnet' is different because it focuses on the poet's enjoyment of nature: he repeats the phrase "I love" three times in the poem, joyously expressing his reaction to the scene he is describing.

Keep comparing the poems all the way through.

Conclusion 8

All these poems use imagery to create vivid descriptions of their different subjects: famine, war, nature's power and nature's beauty. The image that I find most striking is when "The rough bark of humus erupts / knots of potatoes" in 'At a Potato Digging'; this really brings home the fact that what might seem unremarkable to many people is a dramatic event for people who live under the threat of starvation.

Always put in a conclusion.

Sample Essay — Characters

Read through this sample answer for some handy tips on how to write a fantastic essay.
Key words have been highlighted in green — both in the question and the answer.

A Here's an Exam-style Question about Characters

Question 1 Compare the ways characters are portrayed in *Digging* by Seamus Heaney and three other poems, one by Gillian Clarke and any two from the Pre-1914 Poetry Bank.

B Here's an Example of a Plan for this Answer

Plan: poems to write about: Digging, Catrin, Ulysses, The Village Schoolmaster
1) Intro about theme - characters
2) Structure
Digging: shorter verses add impact
Catrin: two verses - past and present
Ulysses: 4 verses, each shows diff emotion
Village: 1 verse, descriptions blend together
3) Language
Digging: rugged, harsh
Catrin: striking, down-to-earth
Ulysses: frustrated, heroic
Village: nostalgic, mysterious
4) Attitudes and Feelings
Digging: admiration
Catrin: mixed feelings
Ulysses: boredom, pride, excitement
Village: respect, fear

5) Conclusion - personal response:
Liked Ulysses because you see his human side

Here's an 'A' Grade Answer to the Question

1 Introduction

Characters are the people whose personalities, emotions or actions are portrayed in a poem. They can be real or fictional. Poets use various techniques to present their characters. In 'Digging', Seamus Heaney admiringly describes his father and grandfather tirelessly digging potatoes, while in 'Catrin', Gillian Clarke writes about her strong and defiant daughter. In Alfred Tennyson's 'Ulysses', we see the character of a heroic warrior who is determined to continue his adventures, whereas 'The Village Schoolmaster' by Oliver Goldsmith is about a more ordinary figure.

Start by talking about the theme.

2 Structure

The structure of these poems is important to the impression we get of the characters. 'Digging' consists of a number of verses of different lengths. The effect of this is to add more impact to the line: "By God, the old man could handle a spade". This description of the poet's father stands out because the verse is only two lines long, and it is right in the middle of the poem. 'Catrin' has a different kind of structure, having just two verses. This allows Clarke to split her depiction of her daughter into memories of when she was born and more recent events — her daughter's "defiant glare" in the second verse comes as no surprise after the description of "our first / Fierce confrontation" in the first verse.

Always keep the theme of the question in mind when you're talking about the structure of the poem.

Sample Essay — Characters

2 Structure

The pre-1914 poems also have fairly irregular structures. The structure of 'Ulysses' consists of four verses of differing lengths. This allows Tennyson to show Ulysses' views about different aspects of his life: his frustration at ruling "a savage race", his determination to continue travelling, his feelings about his son Telemachus, and his motivational speech to his crew. In this way we get a good idea of Ulysses's overall character. 'The Village Schoolmaster', however, is not divided into verses. As in 'Ulysses', different aspects of the character are described, such as his "severe" nature and his many skills, but these merge into each other fluently, rather than being separate.

There's only one part to this question, so compare all four poems throughout your essay.

3 Language

In each poem, the style of language used affects our perception of the characters. Heaney's rugged, harsh language adds to the impression of his father and grandfather being strong, hard-working men; the poet vividly describes his father's "straining rump" as he tirelessly digs. Likewise, the language in 'Catrin' reflects the poet's impression of the character she is describing. The language is striking but down-to-earth. Alliteration and rhyme in "your straight, strong, long / Brown hair" emphasises Catrin's strength and good looks.

Compare the way the poets have used language to present the theme.

In 'Ulysses', the language is often more dramatic. Ulysses's speech is always eloquent, whether he's frustrated, excited or proud. He is at his most impressive when he addresses his crew. He refers to them as "my friends", showing he knows them well, and we also see how brave he is, as, although he is old, he still vows to "sail beyond the sunset". In contrast, the nostalgic, uncertain language in 'The Village Schoolmaster' makes the character appear slightly mysterious, as if people were not quite sure what he was like. We are impressed by "The love he bore to learning", but phrases like "still the wonder grew" add to the general impression that the schoolmaster was a strange man.

Use linking words and phrases like "similarly" and "in contrast".

4 Feelings and Attitudes

The poets' feelings about their characters vary. In 'Digging', the poet has nothing but admiration for his father and grandfather. He is clearly very proud to be related to his grandfather when he tells us how he "cut more turf in a day / Than any other man on Toner's bog". Clarke also has admiration for the character in her poem, but this is mixed in with frustration and possibly even aggression. The poet says she is still "fighting / You off", showing how, despite her admiration for her daughter, she sees her as confrontational and a nuisance.

Back up your points with quotes from the poems.

It'll look good if you can work some quotes into your sentences.

In 'Ulysses', there is also a range of feelings: boredom at the prospect of ruling his people, pride when he thinks of what he has "seen and known" and also for his son, and excitement at his coming travels. The feelings and attitudes in 'The Village Schoolmaster' are less obvious. The narrator seems to respect this character for his knowledge and skills, telling us he spoke in "words of learned length". But the schoolmaster was also rather unpleasant: the children, or "boding tremblers" had to pretend to find his jokes funny so as not to upset him.

Link the feelings and attitudes in the poem to the theme.

5 Conclusion

These poems have an interesting and diverse range of characters. I particularly enjoyed the depiction of Ulysses. Tennyson makes this classical hero seem all the more impressive for the fact that he knows he is not as young and strong as he once was, yet he is still determined to "drink / Life to the lees". I find this truly admirable.

Give a personal response in the conclusion.

Glossary

adjective	A word that describes something, e.g. "big", "fast", "annoying".
alliteration	Where words start with the same letter. It's often used in poetry to give a nice pattern to a phrase. E.g. 'Sally's slipper slipped on a slimy slug.'
ambiguity	Where a word or phrase has two or more possible meanings.
assonance	When words share the same vowel sound but the consonants are different. E.g. "Lisa had a piece of cheese before she went to sleep, to help her dream."
blank verse	Poetry that doesn't rhyme, usually in iambic pentameters.
colloquial	Sounding like everyday spoken language.
compound word	A word that is made up of two or more other words put together, e.g. "flame-red".
consonants	All the letters in the alphabet that aren't vowels.
contrast	When two things are described in a way which emphasises how different they are. E.g. a poet might contrast two different places or two different people.
dialect	Regional variation of a language. People from different places might use different words or sentence constructions. E.g. In some northern English dialects, people might say "Ey up" instead of "Hello".
empathy	When someone feels like they understand what someone else is experiencing and how they feel about it.
enjambement	When a sentence runs over from one line to the next.
iambic pentameter	This is a form of poetry that doesn't rhyme, but usually has a clear metre of ten syllables — five of them stressed, and five unstressed. The stress falls on every second syllable, e.g. "Coral is far more red than her lips' red."
imagery	Language that creates a picture in your mind.
irony	When words are used in a sarcastic or comic way to imply the opposite of what they normally mean. It can also mean when there is a big difference between what people expect and what actually happens.
language	The choice of words used. The language determines the effect the piece of writing will have on the reader, e.g. it can be emotive or persuasive.
layout	The way a piece of poetry is visually presented to the reader. E.g. line length, whether the poem is broken up into different stanzas, whether lines are arranged regularly or create some kind of visual pattern.
metaphor	A way of describing something by saying that it is something else, to create a vivid image. E.g. "His eyes were deep, black, oily pools."
metre	The arrangement of syllables to create rhythm in a line of poetry.
mood	The feel or atmosphere of a poem, e.g. humorous, threatening, eerie.
mythology	A collection of very old stories, often involving gods and heroes. Different cultures have their own mythologies.
narrator	The voice speaking the words that you're reading. E.g. a poem could be written from the point of view of a young child, which means the young child is the poem's narrator.

Glossary

noun	A word for a place, person or thing, e.g. "tree", "air", "Boris", "London".
onomatopoeia	A word that sounds like the thing it's describing. E.g. "buzz", "crunch", "bang", "pop", "ding".
persona	A fictional character or identity adopted by a poet. Poets often create a persona so they can describe things from a different person's point of view, e.g. a male poet might use a female persona.
personification	A special kind of metaphor where you write about something as if it's a person with thoughts and feelings. E.g. "The sea growled hungrily."
phonetic	When words are spelt as they sound rather than with their usual spelling. It's often used to show that someone's speaking with a certain accent.
rhyme scheme	A regular system of rhyming words in a poem, e.g. in 'The Man He Killed', the 1st line of each verse rhymes with the 3rd, and the 2nd rhymes with the 4th.
rhyming couplet	A pair of lines that are next to each other and whose final words rhyme.
rhythm	When sentences or lines have a regular fixed pattern of syllables.
simile	A way of describing something by comparing it to something else, usually by using the words "like" or "as". E.g. "He was as pale as the moon," or "Her hair was like a bird's nest."
sonnet	A type of poem with fourteen lines, and usually following a clear rhyme pattern. There are different popular patterns for sonnets. They will often have ten syllables a line, and end with a rhyming couplet.
stanza	A group of lines in a poem that often share the same rhythm pattern and have similar line lengths. Stanzas can also be called verses.
stereotype	An inaccurate, generalised view of a particular group of people. E.g. A stereotype of football fans might be that they're all hooligans.
structure	The order and arrangement of a piece of writing. E.g. how the poem begins, develops and ends, whether it uses verses or not, whether it has a particular layout, etc.
syllable	A single unit of sound within a word. E.g. "all" has one syllable, "always" has two and "establishmentarianism" has nine.
symbolism	When an object stands for something else. E.g. a candle might be a symbol of hope, or a dying flower could symbolise the end of a relationship.
syntax	The way a sentence is put together so that it makes sense.
theme	An idea or topic that's important in a piece of writing. E.g. a poem could be based on the theme of friendship.
verb	A word that describes something you do, e.g. "run", "talk", "hope".
vocabulary	All the words used in a piece of writing.
voice	The personality narrating the poem. Poems are usually written either using the poet's voice, as if they're speaking to you directly, or the voice of a character, e.g. an elderly man, or a horse.
vowels	Simple — the letters 'a', 'e', 'i', 'o' and 'u'.

Index

Index

The Publisher would like to thank:

Poets:

Gillian Clarke 'October', 'Baby-sitting', 'Mali', 'Cold Knap Lake' and 'Catrin' from *Collected Poems* (1997); 'A Difficult Birth' and 'The Field-Mouse' from *Fivefields* (1998); 'On the Train' from *Making the beds for the dead* (2004), all reprinted by permission of the publishers, Carcanet Press Ltd.

Seamus Heaney 'Storm on the Island', 'Blackberry-Picking', 'Death of a Naturalist', 'Digging', 'Mid-Term Break', 'Follower' and 'At a Potato Digging' from *Death of a Naturalist* (1966); 'Perch' from *Electric Light* (2001), all reprinted by permission of the publishers, Faber and Faber Ltd.

William Butler Yeats 'The Song of the Old Mother' published by permission of A.P. Watt Ltd. on behalf of Michael B. Yeats

Image sources:

Image of Gillian Clarke © photographer Jane Bown

Image of Seamus Heaney © photographer David Levenson/Getty Images

Images of Ben Jonson, William Wordsworth, William Blake, John Clare, Thomas Hardy, Walt Whitman, Robert Browning, Alfred Lord Tennyson and Oliver Goldsmith © Mary Evans Picture Library

Images of William Butler Yeats and Gerard Manley Hopkins © National Portrait Gallery, London

Image of William Shakespeare © Royal Shakespeare Company

Every effort has been made to locate copyright holders and obtain permission to reproduce poems and images. For those poems and images where it has been difficult to trace the originator of the work, we would be grateful for information. If any copyright holder would like us to make an amendment to the acknowledgements, please notify us and we will gladly update the book at the next reprint. Thank you.